A Visit to

With an Account of the Fou_____ ___g_p___

W. Basil Worsfold

Alpha Editions

This edition published in 2024

ISBN : 9789362995926

Design and Setting By
Alpha Editions
www.alphaedis.com
Email - info@alphaedis.com

Contents

PREFACE.

In writing these pages I have had before me a double purpose. First, to present to the general reader an account of what seemed to me to be a singularly interesting country, and one which, while being comparatively little known, has yet certain direct claims upon the attention of Englishmen. Secondly, to provide a book which, without being a guide book, would at the same time give information practically useful to the English and Australian traveller.

In sending this book to the press I have to acknowledge the courtesy of the editors of the *Field* and of *Land and Water*. To the former I am indebted for permission to make use of an unusually interesting quotation from Mr. Charles Ledger's letter to the *Field* on the subject [iv]of cinchona introduction, and also to include a short article of my own on "Horse-racing in Java" in Chapter XII. The latter has kindly allowed me to reproduce an account of my visit to the Buitenzorg Gardens, published in *Land and Water*. My general indebtedness to standard works, such as Raffles' "Java," and Mr. Wallace's "Malay Archipelago," and also to those gentlemen who, like Dr. Treub, most kindly placed their information at my disposal in Java, is, I hope, sufficiently expressed in the text.

Professor Rhys Davids has very kindly read over the proof sheets of the chapter on the Hindu Temples; and I take this opportunity of acknowledging my sense of his courtesy in so doing, and my indebtedness to him for several valuable suggestions.

The spelling of the Javanese names and words has been a matter of some difficulty. The principle I have finally adopted is this. While adopting [v]the Dutch spelling for the names of places and in descriptions of the natives, and thus preserving the forms which the traveller will find in railway time tables and in the Dutch accounts of the island, I have returned to the English spelling in narrative passages, and in those chapters where the reader is brought into contact with previous English works. But I have found it impossible to avoid occasional inconsistencies. In my account of the literature of the island I have kept to the Dutch titles of Javanese works as closely as possible; but I have modified the transliteration in accordance with the usages of English oriental scholars.

W. B. W.

1, PUMP COURT, TEMPLE, E.C.,
November, 1892.

CHAPTER I.
HISTORICAL ACCOUNT UP TO THE PRESENT DAY.

Hindus—Mohammedans—Portuguese—English—Dutch— Legal basis of
Dutch possession—British occupation— Return of Dutch—Culture
system—Eruption of Mount Krakatoa.

In the centre of that region of countless islands termed not inaptly the
"Summer of the World," midmost of the Sunda group of which Sumatra lies
to the west, and Flores to the east, with the fury of the tropical sun tempered
by a physical formation which especially exposes it to the cooling influence
of the ocean, lies the island of Java. Rich in historic remains of a bygone
Hindu supremacy, when the mild countenance of Buddha gazed upon
obedient multitudes, in memorials of Mohammedan, Portuguese, and Dutch
seafaring enterprises, it is a country singularly alluring to the student and
antiquarian. Nor is its present life less interesting. Densely populated by a
simple and refined native race, who live for the most part in the midst of
mountain glories and tropical verdure, itself the best example of a rival and
successful system of colonization, modern Java is no mere tourist's country,
but one which possesses, and always has possessed, special attractions for
the man of science and the political student.

From an immense mass of native tradition the main outlines of the history
of the island can be disentangled with sufficient certainty.

Javanese tradition universally speaks of a personage called Saka, variously
termed warrior, priest, and god, to whom is attributed the introduction of
the arts of civilization, and whose advent marks the opening year of the
native chronology. The first year of Saka corresponds to the seventy-eighth
of the Christian era. There can be no doubt as to the region from which this
extraneous civilization came. Native tradition and the vast religious
monuments of the eastern and central districts alike point to an Indian
colonization and supremacy; for the temples of Java bear the stamp of a
culture and of an artistic and architectural genius superior to that possessed
by a race, the sole record of whose national existence is contained in the
meagre tradition of an immigration from the western lands about the Red
Sea.

Sir Stamford Raffles, in his exhaustive history of Java, gives the names and
dates of the Hindu monarchs, with an account of their conquests and
administrations. But the native chronicles require to be carefully sifted, and
to be supported by the record of the antiquarian remains, which supply an
unfailing basis for, at any rate, the main outlines of the period. The oldest

inscriptions are found on the west side of Buitenzorg, on river stones, and at Bekasi, on the east side of Batavia; they are written in Sanskrit characters of the oldest period, and, by comparison with the inscriptions of British India, indicate the existence of Hindu civilization in Java during the fourth and fifth centuries after Christ. The oldest *dated* inscription in Java (and in the Archipelago) is one bearing date 654 of Saka (A.D. 732). This is now in the museum at Batavia. It contains twelve verses in the Sanskrit tongue, and is about four feet in length by two in width, and about ten inches in depth.

The magnificent temple of Boro-Boedoer, of which Mr. Wallace[1] says, "The amount of human labour and skill expended on the Great Pyramid of Egypt sinks into insignificance when compared with that required to complete this sculptured hill temple in the interior of Java," and which will be separately described with the other religious monuments, was probably erected in the eighth or ninth century. It marks the highest point in the Hindu supremacy, and the time when the influence of Buddhism was supreme. At any rate, we have the witness of Fa Hian, a Chinese traveller, who visited the island in the fifteenth century, to the effect that at this later period "the Brahmins were still very numerous, but the law of Buddha was no longer respected."

The earliest European visitors tell us nothing of the two Hindu kingdoms, Pajajaran and Majapahit, so celebrated in the chronicles. They speak only of Sunda and its port Bantam; and they mention a certain prince, Fateléhan, as completing the Mohammedan conquest in 1524. Raffles, however, following the chronicles, focusses the overthrow of the Hindu supremacy in the capture of the city of Majapahit in 1478 A.D. In spite of the traditions which speak of a long period of fighting, it is probable that the conversion of the Javanese to the new religion was gradual and peaceable, being in the main the result of commerce. The temples, the head-quarters of the old religion, show no traces of violence. They were destroyed, says Dr. Leemans,[2] simply by "carelessness, disuse, and nature," not by a sanguinary war. Long before the Prince Fateléhan conquered the western kingdom of Sunda in 1524, Arab merchants had spread the principles of Islamism among the Javanese. It was just at the time of the establishment of the Mohammedan power that the first Europeans made their way to the island. Portuguese writers say that their people, after the conquest of Malacca in 1511, entered into relations with the inhabitants of Bantam, through Samian, a prince of Sunda, who had formerly lived at Malacca. Lemé, a Portuguese sent by Albuquerque, Captain of Malacca, made a treaty with this Samian, and obtained permission to build a fortress at Bantam on condition that the prince and his subjects were protected from the Moors. In the realization of this object, an expedition was sent by the Portuguese king under command of Francesco de Sa; but before it reached the prince Bantam had been taken by treason, and the Mohammedan power established under Fateléhan. Henceforward the native rulers were Mohammedans, and the list of these sovereigns given by Raffles extends from A.D. 1477 to A.D. 1815.

A PORTUGUESE HOUSE, BATAVIA.

The Portuguese were followed by the Dutch and English after some considerable interval. The first Dutch fleet, under the command of Admiral Houtman, sailed for Bantam in the year 1595. The prince, who was then at war with the Portuguese, allowed them to establish a factory there, and thus the first Dutch settlement in the East Indies was formed. Not long after, the English East India Company (immediately after their incorporation by Queen Elizabeth in 1601) despatched a force under Captain Lancaster. He succeeded in establishing friendly relations with the prince, who sent a letter to the English queen, which is still extant among the state records. This is noticeable as being the first settlement of the East India Company; and as showing that Hindustan, which now means India for most people, was not the original "India" of the company. In the subsequent quarrels between the natives and the Dutch, the English assisted the former so successfully that at one time the Dutch had to enter into a convention with the native chiefs and the English commander, by which they agreed to surrender their fort at Jakatra and evacuate the island. On the conclusion of peace, however, between the Dutch and English in Europe, and on the arrival of reinforcements under Jan Pietersen Koen, they changed their plans, and, instead of retiring from the island, proceeded to lay the foundations of an extensive settlement at Jakatra.

In the following year (1621) the name of Batavia was given to the settlement, and from this period onwards the Dutch continually increased their influence in the island, until in 1749 a deed containing a formal abdication of the sovereignty of the country was secured from the dying *susunan* (or Mohammedan emperor). In this the unfortunate prince "abdicates for himself and his heirs the sovereignty of the country, conferring the same on the Dutch East India Company, and leaving it to them to dispose of in future, to any person they might think competent to govern it for the benefit of the company and of Java."[3] It is by virtue of this deed that the Dutch East India Company, and subsequently the Dutch Colonial Government, became practically landlord of the whole island. Since the Government assumed possession of the soil they have gradually bought up the previously existing rights of the native princes, and in return have guaranteed them certain revenues, which have now become in most cases mere official salaries. Among the rights which the Government secured, by thus becoming landlord of the island, was that of receiving one-fifth part both of the produce and of the labour of the Javan peasants. This fact—that the mass of the Javan natives owed, as it were, feudal services to the Government— explains the comparative ease with which, nearly a century later, the culture system was introduced.

The English settlement at Bantam was withdrawn in 1683, and no effort was made to interfere with the Dutch until the year 1811, when, owing to the conquests of Napoleon in Europe, the island had become a mere French province. In that year a British force reduced Java and its dependencies. During the short period of British occupation (1811-1816) extensive reforms were introduced by Sir Stamford Raffles, the lieutenant-governor. These reforms had for their object the improvement of the condition of the mass of Javan natives, and the liberation of the industries of the island from the restrictions placed upon them by the monopolist policy of the Dutch. Whatever may be the verdict of history as to the practical value of these proposals, the attempt to carry them out has at least left behind such a tradition of British justice as to cause a feeling of profound respect towards the English to be almost universally entertained in the island to this day.

In the settlement effected by the Treaty of London, in 1814, the British Government retained the Cape and Ceylon among the Dutch possessions acquired by conquest in the Napoleonic wars, but Java and its dependencies were restored to their former masters. A right of protectorate, however, over the neighbouring island of Sumatra belonged to the British crown until the year 1872, when it was surrendered in return for equivalent rights on the Gold Coast of Africa. This concession has proved a veritable *damnosa hereditas* to the Government of Netherlands India. The attempt to enforce the newly acquired rights over the Sumatrans resulted in the outbreak of the Atchinese war in 1873, an event which has involved the island of Java in serious financial difficulties, and imperilled the prestige of Holland in the East.

A great part of the special interest which attaches to Java is derived from the fact that it has been the scene of an interesting financial experiment. The history of the introduction of the culture system, and of its gradual abandonment in recent years, is so interesting as to require a separate chapter to itself, and it is only necessary to mention here just so much as is essential for the purposes of a historical sketch. The author of the proposal was General Van den Bosch, who became Governor-General in 1830. The system continued in full operation until the year 1871, when the Home Government passed an Act providing for the gradual abandonment of the Government sugar plantations. By the year 1890 sugar, by far the most important of the Javan industries, was practically freed from Government interference. At the present time it is in debate whether or not the coffee industry should be similarly treated.

This short historical sketch would be incomplete without some mention of an appalling and unique event in the history of the island. On the 27th of August, 1883, the green-clad island of Krakatoa, which rises for some three thousand feet out of the waters which separate Sumatra from Java—the Straits of Sunda—was the scene of a most terrific volcanic discharge. Whole towns were destroyed in both islands; but even more striking than the loss of human life and property is the fact, now satisfactorily established, that the discharge of ashes was so great as to cause a series of extraordinarily brilliant sunsets all over the world, while the force of the tidal wave was such as to affect the level of the water in the river Thames. In travelling from Batavia to Singapore, I was fortunate enough to meet with an officer in the employ of the Netherlands India Steamship Company, who was able to give me an actual narrative of his personal experience of this wonderful eruption. Mr. S—— was at that time second engineer on the steamship *Governor-General Lowden*, belonging to the same company. I cannot do better than close this chapter with his narrative.

"We were anchored off Telokbetong, in Sumatra, when the chief officer and myself observed a dark line out at sea which bore the appearance of a tidal wave. While we were remarking this, the captain (who was just then taking his bath) rushed on to the bridge, and telegraphed to the engine-room to steam slow ahead up to the anchors. I was engaged in carrying out this order when the wave came up to the ship. First she dropped; then heaved up and down for some five minutes. There were three waves. When I came on deck again, the long pier, which had been crowded with Europeans who had come out of the town (they had experienced a shock of earthquake during the night),—this pier, the houses and offices, had disappeared, in fact, the whole town was gone. A Government steamboat lying at anchor (with steam up) in the bay was landed high on the tops of the palm trees in company with some native boats. That was the first intimation we received that Krakatoa was in eruption, and from that time, eight o'clock, onwards through the day the rumbling thunders never ceased, while the darkness increased to a thick impenetrable covering of smoky vapour. Shortly after this we got under way, and proceeded until the darkness made it impossible to go on further. It was while we were thus enveloped in darkness that the stones and cinders discharged by the mountain began to fall upon the ship. In a short time the canvas awning and the deck were covered with ashes and stones, to the depth of two feet, and all our available men were employed in removing the falling mass, which would otherwise have sunk the ship. We had a large number of natives on board, and a hundred and sixty European soldiers. The latter worked with the energy of despair at their task of clearing the deck, in spite of the twofold danger of being burnt and stunned by the hot falling stones. While we were engraved in this struggle, and enveloped in the sheer blackness of a veritable hell, a new and terrible danger came upon us. This was the approach of the tidal wave caused by the final eruption, which occurred about 12.30 to 1 p.m. The wave reached us at 2 p.m. or thereabouts, and made the ship tumble like a sea-saw. Sometimes she was almost straight on end, at other times she heaved over almost on her beam-ends. We were anchored and steaming up to our anchors as before, and as before we managed to escape destruction. All the passengers and the crew gave themselves up for lost, but there was no panic, and the captain handled the ship splendidly throughout. He received a gold medal from the Government in recognition of his indomitable courage in saving the ship and passengers. Well, you can fancy what it was like when I tell you that the captain was lashed with three ropes alongside the engine-room companion, while I was lashed down below to work the engines. The men were dashed from one side of the engine-room to the other.

"When we reached Angier we found no trace—neither a splinter of wood nor a fraction of stone—of the buildings of that once flourishing seaport. At Batavia the water was so dense from the floating lava (the deposit reached fifteen feet in depth) that we made our way to the shore on planks. Telokbetong was closed for three or four months, and on our return to Achin we could not land our passengers. At Batavia the tidal wave had penetrated almost to the town, where in the lower portion the houses were flooded by the Kali Bezar (great river). Business was suspended except by a few determined spirits who worked on by gaslight, so great was the alarm at the darkness and thunderous noises."

Footnotes:

[1] "Malay Archipelago."

[2] "Bôrô-Boedoer Temples," by Dr. C. Leemans, à Leide 1874.

[3] Raffles' "History."

CHAPTER II.
TRAVELLING AND HOTELS.

Area—Climate—Permission to travel—Chief objects of interest—Means of locomotion—Language—Hotels.

Of the many travellers who have written accounts of their visits to Java, not one has been explicit in his directions as to the ways and means of reaching the various interesting objects which he has described. This may partly be accounted for by the fact that there are, indeed, no Titanic difficulties to be encountered. The districts to be traversed are furnished with excellent roads, and in part with railways, contain large and civilized towns, and are inhabited by a peaceable and industrious population. The difficulties, such as they are, can be overcome by the two necessaries for all except the most hackneyed excursions—time and money. In Java the former is, if anything, more important than the latter.

Java—with which is included for all purposes the little island of Madura, lying off its north-eastern coast—is a long narrow island six degrees south of the equator. It is 630 miles long, and averages 100 miles in breadth. Its area is 51,961 square miles, an extent slightly greater than that of England; and the present population reaches a total of twenty-three millions. Like all the islands of the Malay Archipelago, its surface is diversified by great mountains (generally volcanic) and extensive plains. It is poorly supplied with minerals; coal is there, but not in workable quantities; perhaps the only valuable mineral products are the clay, which is made into bricks, earthenware, and porcelain, and the deposits of salt in the Government mines.

On the other hand, the soil is proverbially fertile. The chief products are best exhibited in connection with the four botanical zones into which Junghuhn has divided the island according to elevation:

| I. | From the seaboard to 2000 feet. | Tropical. | Rice, sugar, cinnamon, cotton, maize. |
| II. | From 2000 feet to 4500 feet. | Moderately hot. | Coffee, tea, cinchona, sugar-palm. |

| III. | From 4500 feet to 7500 feet. | Moderately cool. | Indian corn, tobacco, cabbage, potatoes. |
| IV. | From 7500 feet to 12,000 feet. | Cold. | European flora. |

The climate varies in accordance with these zones. Observations made at Batavia (on the coast), the only place where a record covering a sufficient period has been kept, give a mean of 78.69° for a period of twelve years. The monthly mean shows a variation of only two degrees. The period from April to November, when the south-east trade winds prevail, called the dry or east monsoon, is slightly warmer than the remaining six months which make up the rainy season. The heaviest rainfall is in the months of December, January, and February. The chief characteristic of the climate of Java is, therefore, not so much its heat as its equability: it is rarely wet all day long even in the wet season, and at least one shower may be expected each day in the dry.

In spite of its great heat Java is generally healthy, and, in cases of simple bronchitis, the climate is positively helpful. Of course the mountain districts are preferable to the plains, but in the ordinary routes traversed by travellers there are no conditions to be encountered which are adverse to persons in the enjoyment of ordinary health. Buitenzorg (close to Batavia), the summer residence of the Governor-General, a place which is to Dutch India what Simla is to British India, is especially healthy, being some seven hundred feet above sea-level. Tosari, again, in the eastern part of the island, is a recognized sanatorium. It has a capital hotel, and lies at an elevation of six thousand feet above sea-level. This latter place is easily reached in one day from Soerabaia; and close by is Mount Bromo, one of the most active volcanoes in Java, and one which is always covered with smoke. A three-mile walk will give the visitor an opportunity of seeing the boiling crater—a magnificent spectacle. Mount S'meroe, the highest mountain in Java (12,000 feet), is also in the neighbourhood.

The best time to travel is the dry season, April to November, when the nights are cooler and the weather brighter; and, of course, in travelling by carriage, arrangements should be made to avoid proceeding during the hottest part of the day as much as possible.

The Dutch are nothing if they are not methodical, and in order to travel in Java certain formalities, which at first sight appear somewhat formidable, but which are really matters of form, have to be gone through. Any person intending to remain in the island for more than twenty-four hours must register his name with the police, and give them particulars of his age, birthplace, profession, last place of residence, the ship in which he arrived, and the name of its captain. He thereupon receives a document entitled *Toetlakings-kaart* ("admission ticket"), which states that the person so named and described arrived at a certain date, "with the intention of residing in Netherlands India," and that he is permitted, "by authority of the ordinance of March 12, 1872, to reside in any of the chief harbours or ports open for general trade, and also at Buitenzorg." It is signed by the Assistant-Resident of Batavia. This "admission-ticket" is not sufficient to authorize the new arrival to travel in the interior. For this purpose a second and still more imposing document must be obtained. This is an extract from the register of "decisions" of the Governor-General, and is to the effect that the petition of the undersigned So-and-so has been read, and "that the Governor-General has been pleased to grant him permission to travel for six months in Java."

If the visitor wishes to enjoy any sport he will require a third document, signed by the Resident, to entitle him to "import the following weapon and ammunition, namely," his gun, "which is intended for his own use." It will be a relief to the reader to know that in my own case the documents confirming the grant of all these privileges were obtained at the cost of half a crown for stamps.

Batavia, the capital of Java and the seat of government of the Dutch possessions in the East, is distant two hundred and fifty miles from Samarang, and four hundred from Soerabaia, the ports which respectively "tap" the populous central and eastern districts. While these two latter towns are connected by rail with each other, communication with Batavia is maintained at present by steamboats and post-carriages, since there is a break of one hundred and twenty miles—from Garoet, the terminus of the western railway, to Tjilatjap, a port on the southern coast—in the trunk line which is eventually to unite the whole island. Batavia, however, in spite of this drawback, is the natural starting-point for the visitor. In the first place, it is the port of call of the principal steamboat companies which connect Java with Australia, British India, China, and Europe; and in the next, being the seat of government and containing the chief political and scientific authorities, it is the centre from which information and assistance of all kinds may be obtained. In particular, I would recommend a visit to the museum of antiquities at Batavia as an introduction to the study not only of the Hindu remains, but also of the native industries and manner of life.

The subjects of special interest in Java may be grouped under five heads— the Hindu antiquities, the native towns, the plantations, tropical plant-life, and sport. In the case of the three latter, the several neighbourhoods required to be visited are easily accessible from Batavia by the western railway.

Soekaboemi, the centre of the coffee and cinchona plantations, and the head-quarters of the Planters' Association, is fifty miles distant. Buitenzorg, with its famous botanical gardens, is within an hour and a half's journey. Here, in the various Government gardens and plantations, the plant-life of the whole Malay Archipelago is conveniently exhibited, both in its scientific and industrial aspects, and a strangers' laboratory is specially provided for scientific visitors. The Preanger Regencies—the best place for sport—may be described roughly as occupying the southern half of the western portion of the island. The chief towns of this district—Tjandjoer, Bandong, and Garoet—are all connected with Batavia by the same line of railway. Of these, Tjandjoer is the residence of the native prince, the Regent of Tjandjoer, who is the chief patron of horse-racing in Java.

But the largest of the native towns and those in the neighbourhood of which the most important of the Hindu remains are to be found, such as Soerabaia, Samarang, Solo, Djokja, and Magalang, are situated in the centre and east of the island. As I have before explained, the western and eastern railways are not yet connected, and therefore the railway alone will no longer be sufficient to convey the traveller to his basis of operations. In planning his journey to these towns he will have to weigh the relative advantages of three routes, and to consider the opportunities offered by three means of locomotion—railway, steamboat, and post-carriage.

In another place[4] I have given in detail, with full information as to distances and expenses, the three possible routes to the temples from Batavia, and therefore I need speak here only in general terms.

The principal coast towns can be reached by the steamships of the Netherlands India Company (or its successor), which average about 1000 tons, and are said to be fairly comfortable. As the fares are comparatively high, most people will prefer to avoid the discomforts incidental to a steamboat, augmented by the conditions of the place—natives and strange food. In travelling by road very considerable fatigue must be undergone, and of course the expense is greater than that incurred in travelling by rail or steamboat. Also, as in such travelling smaller towns and less-known districts are traversed, it is especially desirable to have a "boy," or native servant (who can talk English), to communicate with the natives in the Javanese and Sundanese dialects, since in the out-of-the-way districts Malay is not understood. The railways are much the same as elsewhere, except that the rate of travelling is slower and the cost of travelling rather more than usual. As part of the railways are held by private companies, there is a slight variation in both of these particulars on different lines. The construction of railways in Java began in 1875. Ten years later there were 261 miles of private, and 672 miles of Government, railways open for traffic. Since then this extent has been increased, but in 1891 the railway system was still incomplete, by reason of the gap between Garoet and Tjilatjap.

There is another important consideration which will affect the choice of routes and of means of conveyance, and that is the question of language. The natives in the big towns and all servants in hotels and private houses speak Malay, which is the official language for communication between them and the Europeans. There is always supposed to be one man in each native village (or campong) who can speak this language. Malay handbooks are published in Singapore, and although such books cannot be *bought*, as far as I know, in Batavia, they can often be *borrowed*; or, failing this, a few necessary phrases can be written down. Such a phrase, for example, as this: *Apa nama ini?* ("What is the name of this?") will serve to supply the place of many vocabularies. The language, which from its soft sounding has been called "the Italian of the Tropics," is very simple, and seems to consist almost exclusively of nouns (*i.e.* substantives, adjectives, and pronouns). The verb "to be" and prepositions are often omitted, *e.g. Pighi bawa ini Tuan X— =* "Go [and] take this [to] Mr. X——" and most substantives can be formed into verbs. Combinations of substantives are used; e.g. *Kreta api* ("fire-carriages") = "railway." Again, many European words are adopted bodily. In *sadoe* a Frenchman will easily recognize a corruption of *dos-à-dos*; *ayer brandy* (or *ayer whisky*), literally "water-brandy," will present no difficulties to the average Englishman. "Butter" is *mentega*, a Portuguese word. The vowels have the same value as in the Continental languages.[5]

It is obvious that the few words and phrases necessary for everyday life can be easily acquired in such a language, and most people will find the process rather amusing than otherwise. If, however, it is desired to escape this trouble, or to gain a more complete knowledge of the ideas of the natives, a "boy" who speaks English can be secured at Batavia, who will act as valet and interpreter.[6] In communicating with the Dutch residents and the European shop-people in the towns, there is no difficulty experienced, since nearly every one can speak English; if not, recourse can be had to French or German.

In addition to obtaining the formal permission to travel already mentioned, in order to see native ceremonies and enjoy big-game shooting, it is necessary to get recommendations to the residents of the native regencies, and in any case it is desirable to have as many private introductions as possible.

But, however well supplied with such recommendations they may be, all travellers are sure to be more or less dependent on hotels. In Java, as in other tropical countries, the hotels are large one or two storied buildings, with rows of rooms opening upon broad verandahs screened with bamboo blinds, and arranged round courtyards planted with trees. The general living-room and the dining-room have one or more sides open to the air, and are arranged with a view to coolness. The style of cooking in Dutch India is different from that in British India, and has one special peculiarity the—*rice table*, which will be described hereafter; and of course there are minor differences, depending upon the conditions of the place and society. To persons who are prepared to enjoy life (and this is the spirit in which one should travel), the little eccentricities and deficiencies will be a source of amusement, and give additional zest to the travelling experience. But no invalid or dyspeptic should enter the portals of a Javan hotel. As for accommodation, suites of rooms can be engaged, but the ordinary traveller has a large bedroom with the proportion of the verandah belonging to it; this latter is fitted with a bamboo screen, table and chairs, and a hanging lamp, and is for all intents and purposes a sitting-room. The bedroom also is furnished with a view of securing coolness; the floor is covered with matting, and the furniture is not very luxurious; its chief feature is a tremendous bedstead. Now, a Javan bedstead is quite *sui generis*, and requires a ground plan. The ordinary size is six feet square. It is completely covered with mosquito curtains, and has no clothes, the broad expanse being broken by two pillows for the head and a long bolster (called a Dutch wife) which lies at right angles to the pillows. This latter is one of the numerous contrivances for securing coolness. The ordinary routine of hotel life is much the same as elsewhere in the island. At half-past six a coolie comes to the door and awakes you, bringing tea or coffee when you want it. Some time subsequently you proceed in pyjamas, or (if a lady) in a *kabaia* (or loose jacket) and *sarong* (native dress) to the bath-room, which is an important feature in every Eastern hotel. Generally speaking, it is not so very much removed from what Mr. Ruskin would desire. It is a large room with bare walls and a marble floor, on which is placed a cistern or jar of water, from which water is taken with a hand-bucket and poured over the bather, who stands upon a wooden framework. The water runs away from the edges of the room, but I never felt *quite* sure that it didn't come back again afterwards. The walls are sometimes decorated with mirrors, and there is often an arrangement for a shower-bath. But very generally the bather has nothing but bare walls and a huge earthen jar such as Aladdin and the forty thieves would use at Drury Lane. At Singapore this same arrangement obtains, and there it is related that a young midshipman, going to the bath-room and being confronted by a bare interior with nothing but the big jar in the middle of it, very naturally concluded that *this* was the bath. He quickly stripped and got into it; but once in he found it impossible to get out again. After vain endeavours, he rolled the big jar over bodily, and, smashing it on the floor, triumphantly emerged from the fragments. His friends afterwards pointed out to him that there was a hand-bucket there, and enlightened him as to its uses.

Breakfast consists of light breads, eggs, cold meat in thin strips, and fruit, and is served about nine. After breakfast any serious business should be accomplished before the great heat of the day sets in. At 12.30 rice-table (or tiffin) commences. This is a serious meal, and must carry you on till eight o'clock in the evening. The first dish, or rather series of dishes, is that from which the meal takes its name—*rice-table*. In partaking of this the visitor first places some boiled rice upon a soup plate, and then on the top of it as many portions of some eight or ten dishes which are immediately brought as he cares to take—omelette, curry, chicken, fish, macaroni, spice-pudding, etc.; and, lastly, he selects some strange delicacies from an octagonal dish with several kinds of prepared vegetables, pickled fish, etc., in its nine compartments. After this comes a salad, some solid meat (such as beefsteak), sweets, and fruit. Finger-glasses are always provided, and one notices that the salt is always moist, and also that it is not customary to provide spoons for that article. At four, or thereabouts, tea is brought to your room. This serves to rouse you from your siesta, and you then proceed (being by this time again in pyjamas) to take your second bath. After that, European garments are worn, and it is cool enough either for driving or walking. The dinner, which is served at eight, is much like an ordinary *à la Russe* dinner, except that there are rather more small vegetable dishes than is customary elsewhere.

In the Hôtel der Nederlanden at Batavia (and there are plenty of others like it) there is something of the life which is described as belonging to the baths in ancient Roman watering-places. Imagine a long courtyard, with deep verandahs, trees only screening you from the opposite side; around you men in pyjamas, with their feet resting on the arms of their easy-chairs, smoking or taking various iced drinks from long glasses; ladies dressed in the beautiful native garment (the *sarong*) and the lace-trimmed white jacket (the *kabaia*), promenading with children. Opposite you is a little Dutch maiden, whose golden hair and white skin contrasts with the dark complexion of her *baboe*, or nurse. She is dressed in a flowing white robe, and is putting on her stockings in the most *negligé* attitude, for it is now time to go out—4 p.m.—while her mother stands by and scolds her. Everywhere coolies are squatting on the ground in their bright garments, or standing busied with the ordinary duties of service, and *baboes* are playing with their little charges. You are yourself dressed in such a way that you would probably feel uncomfortable were you discovered so dressed in your dressing-room at home; but here you feel perfectly at ease—such is the magical effect of climate—whether promenading in your loose garments or reclining in your easy-chair and gazing coolly upon the occupants of the carriages which cross the courtyard. Or perhaps you are engaged in a chaffing-match with one of the native vendors—Chinese, Malay, or Javanese—who are ever ready to persuade you to buy the commonest trifles at the most fancy prices.

The native servants are very quick and willing to do the visitor's commands; indeed, disasters generally arise from an excess of diligence on their part. For instance, in a damp climate it is an excellent general rule for your "boy" to keep your clothes aired by laying them in the sun two or three times a week; but it is a trifle embarrassing to a modest and impecunious person to see the whole of his wardrobe exhibited *urbi et orbi* in front of his room on the verandah. The pyjamas, suspended in airy fashion, floating in the wind; the coats and trousers hung up on strips of wood so that their full extent is exposed to the sun and air; the pair of pumps, on which only last night he had congratulated himself as looking quite smart by gaslight, now standing confessed in all the unseemliness of bulging sides and torn lining; even the domestic slippers too. Yet such was the scene which met my gaze as I returned from breakfast at nine o'clock in the courtyard of the Hotel Belle Vue at Buitenzorg. *Trop de zèle*, I thought.

CHINESE BARBER.

Footnotes:

[4] Appendix.

[5] The combination *oe* is pronounced *ū* (or *oo*).

[6] The cost of such a "boy" is very small (labour being one thing which is cheap in the island). He is paid from 16 to 18 florins (12 florins = £1) a month; and when travelling it is usual to give him a half-florin a day for food, otherwise the hotel charge for servants, one florin a day, must be paid.

CHAPTER III.
THE SYSTEM OF GOVERNMENT AND THE NATIVES.

Dutch possessions in the East—Government—Army and navy—
Administration—Development of natives—Raden Saleh—Native dress—
Cooking and houses—Rice cultivation—Amusements—Marriage
ceremony.

The Netherlands India, as the Dutch possessions in the East are officially
styled, includes the whole of the Malay Archipelago, with the exception of
the Philippine Islands belonging to Spain, part of Borneo in the possession
of the North Borneo Company, and the eastern half of New Guinea, which
is shared by Germany and England. The total area is officially stated to be
719,674 square miles, and the total population 29,765,031. It is administered
by a Governor-General, a Government secretary, and a Council of State
consisting of five members, who are appointed from among the chief Dutch
residents in the island of Java. As all matters of general policy are controlled
by the Secretary for the Colonies, who is a member of the Home
Government, the functions of the Colonial Government are mainly
executive and consultative. So close is the connection that the colonial
estimates for revenue and expenditure have to receive the approval of the
Home Government before they can be carried out. Moreover, the various
Government officials scattered through the Archipelago are responsible to
the Secretary for the Colonies. There are colleges established both in Holland
and in Batavia in which the young men intended for the colonial service can
receive a suitable training.

The physical sanction upon which the Dutch authority rests is an army of
thirty thousand men, composed of Dutch, Germans, Swiss, Italians, and
natives, but officered exclusively by Dutchmen, and a navy of fifty ships. Of
these troops, a large proportion (amounting in 1891 to 16,537) are native.
The head-quarters of the army is fixed at Batavia. There are barracks at
Weltevreden, and at Meester Cornelis in the capital, and additional
accommodation has been recently provided at Buitenzorg. The fleet is
stationed at Soerabaia, a town which possesses the best harbour in Java, and
which is conveniently situated at the other end of the island. There are,
however, a few ships always stationed at Batavia. The greater proportion of
the fleet is composed of the ships of the Netherlands Indian navy, which is
permanently stationed in the Archipelago; but there are among them some
ships belonging to the Dutch navy, which are relieved every three years.

At the present time, the chief occupation of the colonial forces is the
establishment of the Dutch authority in Sumatra. Since 1874 the natives of

Achin have successfully resisted the Dutch, and the Achin war has proved so costly and so disastrous, that the Home Government have ordered the operations of the troops to be confined to such as are purely defensive. Acting under these instructions, the colonial forces have retired behind a chain of forts, and all attempts to advance into the interior have been abandoned. Last year (1891), Baron Mackay, the Secretary for the Colonies, was able to assure the States General that "excellent results were expected from the blockade system," now adopted, and that the Achinese were already beginning to feel the inconvenience of being cut off from their supplies of necessaries, such as opium and tobacco. Java is by far the most important of the islands of the Malay Archipelago. Its population is four times that of the total population of the remaining Dutch possessions in the East. This population is divided as follows (1890):—

Europeans.	Chinese.	Arabs.	Other Orientals.	Natives.	Total.
48,783	237,577	13,943	1806	22,765,977	23,064,086

With the exception of the Chinese, the great retail traders of the Malay countries, almost the entire population of the island is "native." This term includes various branches of the Malay race, of which the chiefs are the Javanese and Sundanese, occupying respectively the east and west of the island. Separate dialects are also spoken by the people of Bantam and Madura. There is little to distinguish the two chief races, except that the Javanese are more warlike and spirited than the Sundanese, who are somewhat more dull and almost entirely agricultural. Speaking generally, the native population of Java is but little inferior in intelligence to the native population of India, while in some respects—in particular, in the readiness shown by the native princes to assimilate European learning and customs, and in a certain artistic sensibility manifested by the whole people—they resemble the inhabitants of Japan.

The majority of the Javanese natives are employed in the cultivation of rice; in work on plantations, sugar, coffee, cinchona, and tea; and in various lesser industries, such as the making of mats and weaving of *sarongs*. They are also by no means unskilful as workers in clay, wood, and metals, and as artisans generally, and are successfully employed by the Government in working the railways and post and telegraph services.

PALACE OF A NATIVE PRINCE.

For purposes of administration the island is divided into twenty-four residencies. Each residency is further divided into districts, and finally into *campongs*, or townships. It will be remembered that when, at the end of the eighteenth century, the Dutch Government took over the island from the East India Company, they received possession of the soil, subject only to such limitations as the company had already imposed upon their ownership. Since that time the Colonial Government has pursued a policy in Java similar to that pursued by the British in India, by which the native princes have been gradually induced to part with their territorial rights and privileges, and to accept in return proportionate monetary compensations. At the same time the services of these "princes" have been utilized in the work of government. As a result of this latter, the sums paid originally as incomes equivalent to the revenues derived from the rights surrendered have now come to be of the nature of official salaries. Most of these regents, as the native princes are called, receive from two to three thousand florins a year; but some one or two, such as the Sultan of Djokja, and the Regent of Bandong, receive as much as seventy or eighty thousand florins. The Dutch have wisely employed as much as possible the social organization which they found in existence, and native authorities and institutions have been supplemented by European officials. In each residency there is, therefore, a double set of officials, European and native. First of all, there is the Resident, who resides at the chief town, and is the head of all officials, European and native. Under him there are Assistant-Residents, contrôleurs, and assistant-contrôleurs. The contrôleur is an official more especially connected with the Government plantations, and the regulation of the industrial relations between the planters and the peasants, or coolies, is an important duty which he fulfils. The Regent is the head of the native officials, but of course inferior in authority to the Resident, whom he calls his "Elder Brother." Under him is an officer called a *patih*, and then *wedanas*, assistant-wedanas, and ultimately the village chiefs, or *loerahs*. In addition to these there is a further official called a *jaksa*, who ranks above the wedanas, and receives information of any offences committed. In the villages the loerahs act as policemen, but in the towns there are regular native policemen, called *oppas*, who also attend on the wedanas. In each residency there is a court of justice, consisting of a president, who is a paid legal official, a clerk of the court, and a *pangoeloe*, or priest, for administering oaths. In this court the jaksa sits as native assessor to the European judge-president. There are superior courts at the three great towns, Batavia, Samarang, and Soerabaia, and a supreme court at Batavia. Murder and crimes of violence are generally rare, but small thieving is common throughout the island.

The religion of the Javanese is Mohammedanism; although Brahmanism still survives in some of the islands of the Archipelago, it has entirely disappeared from Java. Until recent years the Colonial Government have discouraged any efforts directed towards the conversion of the natives to Christianity. The quietism of the Mohammedan creed was regarded as better adapted to supply their religious needs than the doctrines of the missionaries.

Of late years, however, a more generous policy has prevailed. As the mass of the Javanese regard the native princes as traitors and apostates, the Arab priests and hadjis have come to be recognized as the popular leaders. It is they, and not the princes, who now form the dangerous element. The priests are jealous of European influence, and are ready to incite the natives to revolt if occasion offers, but in any outbreak the native princes are the first to be attacked. A revolt in Bantam had occurred some twelve months before the date of my visit (1890). In return for some injustice, the Resident and his wife and children were put to death by mutilation. The village in which this took place was near Serang, the capital town of Bantam, and only seventy miles from Batavia, and military assistance was obtained from both of these places. The troops from Serang arrived in time to find the body of the Resident's wife still heaving with the action of breathing. Fifty or sixty of the natives were brought to justice for this murder, and six of the ringleaders were shot. I was told that there were numerous secret societies existing in the country, controlled by the Mohammedan authorities in Arabia, and absolutely hidden beyond the reach of the Government.[7]

The question of the moral and mental development of the Javanese natives is one which has lately been much discussed, both in Java and in Holland, and the result has been that the Colonial Government is now fairly pledged to a humanitarian policy. The large sum annually appropriated in the colonial budget to the purposes of public instruction, is a sufficient evidence of the reality of the desire now manifested by the Dutch to give the natives of Java full opportunities for the education and training necessary for technical and industrial progress. There can be no doubt as to the capacity of the natives to benefit by such advantages. When D'Almeida visited the island thirty years ago, he paid a visit to Raden Saleh, a native artist, who had been sent to Holland to be educated there at the expense of the Colonial Government. He had lived for twenty-three years in Europe, residing both in that country and in Germany, and following the profession of an artist. He was chiefly distinguished as an animal-painter, and made such progress in art that he was commissioned by the late Prince Consort to paint two pictures for him, illustrative of Javan life and scenery. Raden Saleh subsequently returned to his native country, and D'Almeida found him residing in an artistically furnished house with large and beautiful gardens near Batavia. In the course of this visit he was asked whether there were any other Javan artists who had attained similar proficiency. He replied, "Café et sucre, sucre et café, sont tout-ce qu'on parle ici. C'est vraiment un air triste pour un artiste."

The artistic perception inborn in the Javan natives is nowhere more clearly manifested than in the colour and form of their dress. Nothing impresses the visitor more quickly or more pleasantly than the gay and graceful groups which throng the streets or roads. The light cottons and silken cloths which the natives wear are admirably suited to the climate, and an exquisite taste seems to govern the selection of colours and the fashion of wearing their garments. Both men and women alike wear the *sarong*, a long decorated cloth wound round the lower limbs and fastened at the waist; over this the former wear a *badjoe*, or short open jacket, and the latter a *kabaia*, or cloak, closed at the waist by a silver pin (*peniti*), and reaching down almost to the bottom of the sarong. Over the right shoulder is gracefully flung a long scarf called a *slendang*, used by mothers to carry their babies, and by the men as a belt when they are engaged in any active work. A square cloth (*kain kapala*) is worn on the head by men; it is folded in half diagonally, and then folded over and round the head until it looks much like a turban. On the top of this a wide straw hat (variously shaped) is carried, to protect the wearer against the sun. The women, on the contrary, wear nothing but their glossy black hair, or carry a bamboo umbrella if they wish for a similar protection.

The native weapons are the bamboo spear, and the short wavy sword called a *kriss*; but the only arm they carry nowadays is a *golok*, or straight piece of iron with a handle and sheath, used for lopping off boughs and cutting wood. The better class of natives use European furniture, but the ordinary peasants and artisans, who live in a bamboo cottage, use nothing but a single bed on which the whole family sleep, and a chest for clothes, both made, like the house, of bamboo.

KOMPOR.

WOMAN COOKING RICE.

The staple diet is rice and dried fish, with vegetables and fruits: cakes and pastry are rare luxuries, and purchased at the market or from itinerant vendors. The cooking arrangements are very simple. Nearly everything is cooked in a *priok*, or frying-pan, which is heated over a *kompor*, or stove of earthenware, or on bricks on a flat stove raised from the ground. In both cases charcoal is burnt, being made to burn brightly by a fan. The rice (which is to them what bread is to us) is not *boiled*, but *steamed*. A copper vessel (*dang-dang*) is filled with hot water, and the rice is then placed in a cone-shaped bamboo basket (*koekoesan*), which is placed point downwards into the vessel and covered with a bamboo or earthenware top (*kekep*). The dang-dang is then placed over the fire either in the *kompor* or on the bricks.

Rice culture is the natural pursuit of the Javanese or Sundanese native. Coffee, sugar, and tea he cultivates on compulsion for wages with which to pay his taxes. Now the land of Java is divided into two classes, land capable of being inundated by streams or rivers called *sawah*, and land not so inundated called *tegal*, or *gaga*. On the latter only the less important crops, such as mountain rice or Indian corn, are grown. On sawah land the rice is grown in terraces, which are so arranged that, without any machinery for raising or cisterns for storing the water, a perfectly natural and perpetual supply is gained from the high mountains, which serve here the same useful purpose that the great river Nile does in Egypt. The small fields are worked with the *patjoel*, a sort of hoe, and the large with the plough (*wloekoe*), and then inundated. After ten or fifteen days they are hoed again, so that any places not reached by the plough or hoe may be laboured, and the intervening banks kept free from weeds and consequently made porous. The large sawahs are also harrowed with the *garoe*; and, finally, small trenches are cut for the water to flow from one terrace to another. When the earth has thus been worked into a mass of liquid mud, the young plants are transplanted from the beds in which they have been sown about a month previously, and carefully placed in this soft mud. Inundation is necessary until the rice is nearly ripe, which is naturally about August or September. It is reaped with a short knife called *ani-ani*, with which the reaper cuts off each separate ear with a few inches of the stem; and the ears are then threshed by being placed in a hollow tree trunk and there stamped with a *toemboekan*, a heavy piece of wood with a broad end. The lands are ploughed, harrowed, and weeded by the men, but the transplanting, reaping, and threshing is done by women.

A curious circumstance in rice-cultivation is the fact that side by side the crops may be seen in each of the separate stages, planting and reaping often going on simultaneously. Beside the rice, a crop of beans or sweet potatoes is grown in the year, and the flooded terraces are also utilized as fish-tanks, in which gold-fish are grown to the length of a foot and a half and then eaten. They are brought to the market in *water*, and so kept fresh, and, if not sold, are of course returned to their "pastures" again.

The sawah plough is an interesting study. It is made in three pieces—the pole (*tjatjadan*); the handle (*patjek*), which fits into the iron-shod share (*singkal*). To this is attached a crosspiece or yoke (*depar*), fitted with a pair of long pegs coming over the necks of the oxen or buffaloes, and a crosspiece hanging under their necks and fastened to the yoke by native cord. The ploughman holds the tail of the plough with the left and the rod-whip (*petjoet*) with the right hand. He drives and directs the big lumbering beasts by words or by a touch of the rod. To make them go "straight on," he calls out, *Gio gio kalen*; "Turn to the right" is *Ghir ngivo*; "To the left," *Ghir nengen*; "Stop" is *His his*; and whenever they (or horses) incur the displeasure of their drivers, they are invariably brought to a better mind by hearing an unpronounceable exclamation something like *Uk uk*.

A BULLOCK CART.

Another natural industry in which the Javanese are particularly skilful is the making of mats. There are many varieties. A light sort of floor-covering is made from the leaves of the wild pine-apple (*pandan*); a stronger kind is the *tika Bogor*, or Buitenzorg matting, which is made from the bark of a species of palm, and which is used to cover walls and ceilings. Beside these, matting is made from rushes and from the cane imported from Palembang, in Sumatra; while for the walls of the houses a heavy matting of bamboo strips is used. The weaving of sarongs is practised by the women all over Java, and the cooking and household utensils, made both in copper and earthenware, indicate by their forms a considerable taste. The Javanese carpenters are also very clever, and both they and the Malays are skilful in imitating any European designs which are handed to them. In spite, however, of this natural aptitude for higher industries, the great mass of the native population are compelled by the present commercial system to remain mere peasants. Even so the cheapness and simplicity of the means of life prevent them from being a joyless race. A plantation cooly generally has two days in the week on which he does no work.

The public feasts are numerous, the chief being the *Taon Baru*, or New Year, which falls at the end of the fasting month, which varies from year to year. In 1890 it lasted from April 21 to May 21. During this month the chiefs and the better class abstain from eating or smoking from sunrise to sunset. Every village has its market once a week or thereabouts, and after this there is generally a *wayang*, or puppet show, and some mild amusement. The wayang is the most important of the native amusements; for the theatre is a rare luxury, and confined chiefly to the towns or to the courts of the native princes. It is a very simple business—far beneath a punch-and-judy show in point of art, but the audience watch the puerile display for five or six hours without intermission. The theatre consists of pantomimic representations, with which is mingled a ballet, the basis of which is ancient tradition. The following story (which I have condensed from D'Almeida's book) is a specimen. A certain King Praboe Sindolo of Mendang Kamolan, feeling tired of the vanities of the world, retired to a hut, where he lived in prayer and fasting. While thus living he was visited by a tempter, who sought to rekindle his desire for the good things of this life. Thereupon Praboe sent for a large bird and four vestal virgins to defend him against the evil spirit. By a miracle he transformed himself into a flower, around which the vestal virgins danced. By chance, however, a princess passed that way, and, seeing a vase with beautiful flowers therein, she chose and gathered one, which she carried to her home. This she placed in water, when, to her surprise, it suddenly was transformed into a young and graceful man. Even as she had cared for him did Praboe care for her, and forthwith he became her lover, and cared nothing any longer for the fasting and the cave.

Much of the Javan festivity is connected with the marriage ceremony, which is always an occasion of feasting, greater or less, in proportion to the wealth of the bride and bridegroom. There is a procession and music, but the actual ceremony is very simple, although the accessory festivities appear to be capable of almost indefinite extension. Barrington D'Almeida, who visited the island in 1861, thus describes the scene[8] which he witnessed in a house filled with guests:—

"On either side of the front room, on white Samarang mats, were seated the elders of the village, priests, various friends, relations, and acquaintances, all squatted cross-legged. Cups of tea, *à la Chinoise*—that is, without milk or sugar—were placed on handsome trays before each guest, as well as betel nuts, cakes, a quantity of *rokos*, and other native delicacies.... Followed by several of the guests, we entered another room, which was very gaudily decorated, and furnished with a low bed, the curtains of which were of white calico, ornamented with lace, gold, silver, beads, and coloured bits of silk. At the foot of this bed was a platform, raised about half a foot from the ground, on which was spread a spotless white mat, with several bronze trays containing cakes, etc. Whilst we were inspecting this apartment we were startled by the din of voices, followed by the sound of music, which, from its peculiar character, was too near to be agreeable. 'The bride is come,' said Drahman. The crowd was so great that it was some minutes before we could catch a glimpse of her. Our curiosity was at length gratified, while they were pouring water upon her small naked feet. After this ceremony an elderly man, who, I was informed, was one of her relatives, carried her in his arms to the inner room, and placed her on the platform, where she sat down on the left side of the bridegroom, who had followed her in. She had a rather pleasing expression, but was much disfigured by a yellow dye, with which her face, neck, shoulders, and arms were covered, and which effectually concealed her blushes.

"Her dress was very simple, consisting of a long sarong of fine *batek*, passing under both arms and across the chest, so that, though her shoulders were quite naked, her bosom was modestly covered. This garment reached nearly down to the young bride's ankles, and was confined round the waist by a silver 'pinding.' Her hair was arranged in the usual Javanese style, with the addition that on the knob at the back of the head rested a kind of crown made of beads and flowers.

"On the left side of the girl sat an old, haggard-looking woman, the waksie, or bridesmaid, on whose shoulders, according to the wedding etiquette of the Javanese, rests no small share of the responsibility.... She is expected to adorn the bride in the most attractive manner, so as to please her husband and the assembled guests; and she superintends all the ceremonies during the celebration of the wedding.... The bridegroom, like his bride, was yellow-washed down to the waist; his eyebrows were blackened and painted to a point; he wore a variegated batek sarong, fastened round the waist with a bright silk scarf, through the folds of which glittered the gilt hilt of a kriss. His hair fell on his back in long thick masses, whilst a conical-shaped hat, made of some material resembling patent leather, was placed on the top of his head. On one side of him was seated his *waksie*, or best man, a boy dressed very much like himself. I was told that the parents of the young couple were absent, as, according to the usual custom in this country, their presence is not expected at the wedding ceremony."

It is interesting to know that the ceremony by which the marriage tie is dissolved is as simple as the marriage ceremony is elaborate. All that is necessary is the consent of the parties; no discredit is involved nor any suffering incurred, and the Arab priest performs the divorce service for a sum so trifling as half a florin! Probably the cheapness of food, and the ease with which life can be supported generally in such a country and climate, is the cause of this laxity of the marriage tie. As a Mohammedan, a Javan peasant is permitted to have as many as four wives, but he can rarely afford more than one, or two at the most.

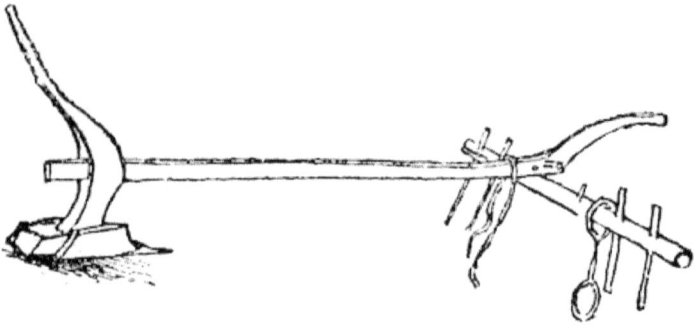

A SAWAH PLOUGH.

CHAPTER IV.
BATAVIA.

Tanjong Priok—*Sadoes*—Batavia—Business quarter—Telephoning—
Chinese Campong—Weltevreden— Waterloo Plain—Peter Elberfeld's
house—Raffles and Singapore.

When the prosperity of the Dutch East India Company was at its height, the
city of Batavia[9] was justly entitled the "Queen of the East." Apart from the
fact that this place was the centre and head-quarters of the company, it was
the emporium through which the whole commerce of the East passed to and
from Europe. The Dutch possessions of Ceylon, the Cape of Good Hope,
and the Moluccas depended for their supplies on Java. Not only were the
European imports, iron, broadcloth, glass-ware, velvets, wines, gold lace,
furniture, and saddlery destined for these settlements received here in the
first instance, but similar imports intended for China, Cochin, Japan, and the
Malay islands were also reshipped from this port into the native boats which
conveyed them to those several countries. Similarly, the wealth of China and
the East was first collected upon the wharfs of Batavia before it was finally
despatched to the various ports of Europe and America.

Since the foundation of the town, the seashore has silted up to such an extent
that the original harbour of Batavia, in which the Dutch East Indiamen of
the seventeenth and eighteenth centuries lay at anchor, has been abandoned,
and a new port has been constructed at a point six miles to the eastward. The
harbour works at Tanjong Priok, as the present port of Batavia is called, and
the railway which connects the port and town of Batavia, are one among
many improvements set on foot in the island since the inauguration of a
public-works policy by the Colonial Government in 1875. Ocean steamships
of 4000 and 5000 tons burden can now be berthed at these wharfs, and there
is a constant and convenient service of trains between the port and the town.
Even to-day the presence of superannuated Dutch warships and quaint craft
from China and the Malay islands relieves the monotony of the vast hulls of
the steamships of the British India, the Messageries Maritimes, and the
Netherlands India Companies.

I was agreeably surprised at the size and convenience of the station at
Tanjong Priok. The booking clerk, who was, I think, a Chinaman, seemed to
know the ways of strangers, and I and my fellow-passengers had no difficulty
in taking tickets for Batavia. The line passed through groves of cocoa-nut
palms, intersected with canals. Everything was quaint and interesting, the
canal boats, the buffalo ploughs, the gaily-feathered birds,—all revealed a
new and delightful phase of life and nature. We were immensely struck with
the appearance of a native cutting grass. He had a hooked blade of steel

fastened to a long handle, forming an instrument not unlike a cleek or other golf-stick. This he slowly swung round his head, and each time it touched the ground cleared about three inches of grass. The thing looked too absurd. We all wanted to get out and ask him how long he expected to be mowing that strip of grass by the canal-side.

While I was on board ship I had been fortunate enough to borrow a Malay phrase-book from a man who had visited the Archipelago before, and during the voyage to Batavia I had amused myself with copying out some of the phrases and committing them to memory. On landing I found these few phrases extremely useful, and I mention the fact by way of encouragement, and in case any other traveller should be inclined similarly to beguile the tedium of the voyage. He will have his reward.

When Mr. Wallace visited Java in 1861, he tells us he found no conveyances in Batavia except "handsome two-horse carriages," costing something under a sovereign a day. He justly complains of the expensiveness of these vehicles, and also of the cost of the post-carriages which then formed the sole means of locomotion in the interior of the island. To-day things are greatly improved. To say nothing of the railway system which connects the large towns in the east and west, Batavia is provided with an excellent tramway, and with a capital supply of small vehicles called *sadoes*.

THE KING'S PLAIN, BATAVIA.

The sadoe is the hansom of Java. It is a small two-wheeled carriage, in which the seats are placed back to back (hence the name, which is a corruption of dos-à-dos), and which is furnished with a square top to keep off the sun. It is drawn by one (or two) of the sturdy little horses bred in the island. At a pinch these vehicles will hold four, but two is enough. Ordinarily the driver sits in front, and the "fare" in the more luxurious seat behind. Thus weighted the country-breds go at a very smart pace; nor is there any complaint to be made in respect of the drivers. They are generally very civil, and their charges are very moderate.

I was told a story which illustrates the docility of the sadoe drivers, and the cleverness with which they can trace and identify their "fares."

An English officer from Singapore, whom we will call Brown, was visiting Batavia, and had occasion, in the course of his visit, to drive in a sadoe from the old town to a friend's house in Weltevreden. For some reason or other he became annoyed with the driver, and, having ejected him, proceeded to drive himself. As it was night, he soon became entangled in the maze of streets. At last he reached the large open space called the King's Plain. He was now close to his destination. The only difficulty was to get rid of the sadoe. In order to do this he drove into the middle of the plain. He waited until the horse began to graze quietly, and then "made tracks" as quickly as might be for his friend's compound. Ultimately he returned to his hotel. The first thing Brown saw, when he got up the next morning, was sadoe, driver, and horse waiting outside his verandah in the courtyard. He grew pale with thoughts of the police; but no, the driver only wanted his fare, which was two florins. Having received this, he retired smiling and contented.

There was a crowd of these sadoes waiting outside the station at Batavia, in one of which I made my way to the Hôtel der Nederlanden.

Batavia may be divided (like all Gaul) into three parts. First, there is the business quarter, the oldest, where the houses are tall and built in the style still prevalent in the warm countries of Europe, with balconies and verandahs and widely projecting eaves, and where the streets are narrow. Then there is the Chinese Campong, which, with the adjacent streets, occupies the central portion of the town, containing the bulk of the population closely packed in their curious dwellings. And, lastly, there is Weltevreden, the Dutch town, where the officials, the military, and the merchants reside. The town is traversed from end to end by the railway, which passes through from Tanjong Priok to Buitenzorg and Bandong; and by the tramway, which runs from the town gate in the north to the statue of Meester Cornelis in the south. It is also divided by the stream called the Kali Bezar, or Great River, and intersected by numerous canals. The pavements are of red brick, and the roads covered with a reddish dust; indeed, the prevailing tone of the whole place is a warm red-brown, varied by salmon-pink and green masonry, and generously interspersed with bright yellow, deep crimson, and olive-green foliage, though not unfrequently a spreading waringin tree or a group of feathery palms overtops the general mass. Additional colour is given by the natives, who are clothed in light cottons and silken stuffs of delicate tones and graceful shapes, carried with an easy carelessness and unfailing novelty of combination. Sometimes they are gathered into dark brown masses round the base of some one of the many bridges which span the river or canals, prepared for the luxury of the tropics—an afternoon bathe.

BRIDGE LEADING TO THE PAZER BAROE, BATAVIA.

All three quarters are possessed of a separate beauty. The elaborately carved pediments and ponderous doors, the heavy balconies and eaves of the houses, give an old-world quaintness to the first, which is enhanced by the crowd of many-shaped and variously coloured boats that line the quays that front the offices on either side of the Great River. Nothing could be more delightful than the setting of the red-tiled roofs, with their dragon-decorated ridges and parapets, on the wooden trellis fronts and canvas blinds of the Chinese houses. Weltevreden, too, is not without attractions. The broad porticoes of dazzling white, with their Ionic columns and marble floors, are often set in a fair surrounding of green trees. The compounds and gardens are always verdant, and sometimes radiant with bright-leaved shrubs and flowers. Especially the broad green-covered squares and the wide roads arched with noble trees speak of coolness and repose in a hot and weary land. On the outskirts of the town, along the country roads, where the cocoa palm and banana plantations begin, are the bamboo cottages of the Sundanese natives.

But it is after nightfall that this place becomes a veritable fairyland. The open porticoes of the Dutch houses are seen to be thronged with gaily dressed people, the ladies often still wearing the sarong, and looking like Æneas' mother—

"Proved to be a goddess by her stately tread,"

and in harmony with the pillars and pediments about them. Everywhere lights gleam through foliage, and ever and again, through an air instinct with electric movement and heavy with perfumes, strains of music reach the ear from the open doorways, or are wafted in the distance from one of the numerous military bands, which are ever "discoursing sweet music" to the society of the capital. In the centre of the town the native streets look, to the European eye, like a perpetual festival. Outside the doors are gathered in groups the various inhabitants—Chinese, Malay, or Sundanese, some clanging cymbals and other strange instruments of music, others seated round fires, eating baked cakes or fruits and other frugal dainties. Meanwhile the streets are alive with the rush of numerous cahars[10] and sadoes, drawn by the agile native pony, and with itinerant vendors, who, bearing their baskets suspended from their shoulders by the *pikulan*, or cross-piece, each with a lamp fixed to the rearmost basket, flit to and fro noiselessly on their bare feet.

The business quarter, like the "city" in London, is thronged with merchants and carriages, carts and coolies, and all the machinery of commerce, in the daytime, and entirely deserted at night. The merchants keep their offices open from nine till five, and, in spite of the great heat, work all through the day, with the exception of an hour or so for "tiffin." By this arrangement the early morning and late afternoon, the only time when open-air exercise is possible, is left available for riding or walking. In spite of the romantic exterior of the place, Batavia is not ill-supplied with modern improvements. The tramway system, in which smoke and heat are avoided by the use of a central boiler from which steam is taken for the different locomotives, is especially well suited to the requirements of the climate. The telephone, again, is in constant use both in offices and private houses, although the confusion of languages—Malay, Dutch, and English—makes it a little difficult sometimes to work it. I remember once asking the landlord of the Hôtel der Nederlanden to telephone to a man in the town that I was intending to go to Buitenzorg on the following morning, and the terrible difficulty I had to get him to convey my name to the clerk at the other end.

After ringing up the central office (which is worked by Malays) and getting the connection he wanted, he said—

"Mr. X——?"

"No."

"Mr. X—— is not there" (to me).

"All right," I said; "tell the clerk to tell Mr. X——"

But the telephone was now shut off, and the process of connecting had to be gone through again.

"Tell Mr. X—— What is your name?"

"Worsfold," I said.

"Versfolt?"

"Yes."

"Tell Mr. X—— that Mynheer Versfolt——"

"Who?" (from the other end).

"Mynheer Versfolt."

"Who?"

"Versfolt."

"Who?"

"How you spell it?" (to me).

I spelt it.

"Mynheer V-e-a-s-f-o-l-t. Veasfolt, *Veasfolt*, VEASFOLT."

Here he appealed to a Dutch gentleman who could speak English, and wrote down the name, W-o-r-s-f-o-l-d.

"Tell Mr. X—— that Mynheer—— Listen, I will spell it—W-o-r," etc.

"Oh, never mind; tell him that the Englishman is going to Buitenzorg to-morrow."

"The English gentleman is going to Buitenzorg to-morrow."

"What Englishman?"

"Mynheer Veasfolt."

"Who?"

"Mynheer Veasfold. I will spell it—W-o-r," etc.

"Yes; what about him?"

"Tell Mr. X—— that Mynheer Veasfolt——"

"Who?"

"Oh, never mind," I said; "Mr. X—— will understand."

But the polite landlord was not satisfied. "It is no trouble; I will tell him."

Then I went away in haste, as the process had already occupied half an hour, and I was telephoning to avoid delay. Five minutes later I passed the bureau. The landlord was still at that wretched instrument. I hurried by without daring to look up, fearing that I should be appealed to again. I dared not even ask whether the message ever reached the office or not.

Beside the town gate—a massive stone arch, with two large iron images on either side, remnants of early victories over the kings of Bantam—there are two buildings of interest in this (business) quarter of the town, the *stadthaus*, or town hall, and the town church. The former is just such an old Dutch edifice as might be seen in any of the towns of Holland, standing in a tree-planted space. In it are the offices of the Resident and the police authorities. The *landraad*, or county court, also holds its sittings here; and on the stone terrace in front of the building, the town guard (a native force armed with lances or picks, and therefore called "pickiniers") are generally to be seen drilling. The town church is across the river, on the road to Tanjong Priok. It is given up to a half-caste congregation, but its walls are lined with memorial tablets of former governors, and there are some interesting monuments outside. According to a wooden tablet within, it was built between the years 1693 and 1695 by Pieter Van Hoorn. It contains some handsome silver candelabra and a richly gilt pulpit, and in the vestry there are some handsome old chairs.

The native quarter is remarkable for the picturesque medley of its people and their houses. There are also in the Chinese Campong many fine private houses, which are furnished with courtyards, and elaborately finished. In the decorations of the roof the favourite form of the Chinese dragon is constantly repeated, and extraordinary effects are produced by a sort of mosaic work, with which the spaces over the doorways and windows are filled, and which has a shiny surface almost like majolica ware.

Weltevreden has many handsome buildings, and some which are interesting. Most of them are grouped round the two great squares or parks, the King's Plain and the Waterloo Plain. The former is lined by four magnificent avenues of tamarind trees (*Poinciana regia*), which form a graceful arch of small-leaved foliage, broken here and there by a still wider-spreading waringin tree. On the west side stands the museum, which contains a very perfect collection of the antiquities and industries of the island. There is also a library, and new buildings are in course of erection. It is governed by a directory, which consists in full of eleven members, who have power to fill up any vacancies which may occur. There is a president, a vice-president, a secretary, and a librarian. This latter gentleman is generally to be found at the museum, and a little conversation with him, and a few hours spent in the ethnological and antiquarian sections, form the very best commencement of a tour through the island. Directly opposite the museum is the Weltevreden station and the great black dome of the Dutch church. This latter is noticeable as being the place where the few people who do go to church in Batavia attend, and where marriages are solemnized after the preliminary ceremony at the registrar's.

THE WATERLOO PLAIN, BATAVIA.

The Waterloo Plain is not nearly so large as the King's Plain. On two sides it is lined by officers' bungalows; and the east side is occupied by a large pile of Government offices, called the Palace, and by the military club, the *Concordia*. In front of these buildings there are some prettily laid out gardens, in the centre of which is a statue of Jan Pietersen Van Koen, the first Dutch Governor of Batavia. In the centre of the plain is the monumental pillar from which it takes its name. It consists of a round column with a square base, some forty feet in height, surmounted by a Belgian lion. On the base the following inscription is to be read in plain Roman characters and excellent Latin:—

"In æternam, celeberrimæ diei duodecimæ ante Kalendas Julii MDCCCXV, memoriam, quo, fortitudine et strenuitate Belgarum eorumque inclyti ducis

Wilhelmi, Frederici, Georgi Ludovici, principis arausiaci, post atrocissimum in campis Waterlooæ prœlium stratis et undique fugatis Gallorum legionibus PAX ORBIS RELUXIT...." [William Frederick Charles, Vice-king of India, erected this monument in the year 1827.] "To the perpetual memory of that most famous day, *June 20, 1815,* on which, *by the resolution and activity of the Belgians and their famous General, William Frederich George Ludovic, Prince of Luxemburg,* after a terrible conflict on the plains of Waterloo, when the battalions of the French had been routed and scattered on every side, the peace of the world dawned once more."

Most people will admit that the facts of the famous victory are scarcely detailed with sufficient accuracy by the inscription. And, indeed, the American gentleman who accompanied me on my visit remarked that "he guessed the *lion* at the top was on the whole inferior in size to the *lyin'* at the bottom of the pillar."

Just outside this plain, and opposite one of the small bridges which leads into the native street termed *Pazer Baroe,* is the theatre, which is the most picturesque of the modern buildings of Batavia.

In the main road which leads through that part of the town which covers the site of the original Sundanese capital, Jakatra (meaning "the work of victory"), there is a desolate-looking house which the visitor will do well to include in his archæological investigations. Over the walled-up entrance of this house the remains of a skull spiked on a pike are still to be seen. Underneath is a tablet with the following inscription:—

"In consequence of the detested memory of Peter Elberfeld, who was punished for treason, no one shall be permitted to build in wood or stone, or to plant anything whatsoever, in these grounds from this time forth for evermore. Batavia, April 22, 1722."[11]

This Peter Elberfeld was one of the many natives who conspired from time to time against the Dutch. According to Raffles, the Dutch administration of Java was distinguished from the very first by a "haughty assumption of superiority, for the purpose of overawing the credulous simplicity of the natives, and a most extraordinary timidity, which led them to suspect treachery and danger in quarters where they were least to be apprehended." But large allowances must be made for the precarious position of a handful of Europeans living in the midst of a hostile and numerous population. In the case of the conspiracy in question, the historical outlines of the story are tinctured by an element of romance.

Peter Elberfeld was a half-caste who had acquired considerable wealth, but who was possessed by an intense hatred of the Dutch. Uniting the native princes in a league, he formed a conspiracy to extirpate the entire white population of the island by concerted massacres. When his plans were fully formed and ready for execution, an unexpected circumstance revealed the plot and brought destruction upon the chiefs of the conspiracy. Elberfeld had a niece living with him, who, so far from sharing her uncle's hatred of the Dutch race, had secretly fallen in love with a young Dutch officer. Knowing her uncle's aversion to their foreign masters and jealousy of their power, she did not dare to ask for his consent to the marriage. At last she arranged to elope with her lover. On the night previous to that fixed upon for this event she was unable to sleep, from a feeling of remorse at conduct which seemed ungrateful to one who had at least been indulgent and affectionate to her. As she stood upon the verandah, looking out upon the darkness of the night, she became conscious that some persons, unseen in the darkness, were moving around her. She made her way in alarm to her uncle's chamber, but found it empty. She then went to the dining-room. The door of this room was shut, but, bending down, she perceived that the room itself was filled with people, and listened to their whispered consultations. Overwhelmed with horror at the cruel nature of the conspiracy, and at the terrible ceremonies by which they bound themselves at the same time to mutual loyalty and vengeance on their enemies, she yet hesitated to betray her uncle. Finally love for her betrothed prevailed, and she communicated the particulars of the conspiracy to him. He at once informed the Dutch authorities. On the following night—the night fixed for the elopement—Elberfeld's house was surrounded, and the conspirators were captured as they were on the point of departing to their various stations. Most of the native princes were punished by mutilation, but Elberfeld was reserved for a signal vengeance. Each of his arms and legs were tied respectively to one of four horses, which were then driven by lashes of whips in four different directions. Finally his head was severed from the trunk of his body and impaled. To this day it remains a ghastly memorial of the turbulent past. The most unsatisfactory part of the story is the fact that the girl who had made such sacrifices in her lover's behalf was after all not permitted to be his bride.

The population of Batavia is, in round numbers, 110,000. Of these 7000 are Europeans. In respect of total population it is inferior to Soerabaia, the eastern capital, which has 140,000 inhabitants. There are, however, fewer Europeans at Soerabaia than at Batavia. Samarang, which ranks third in size, has a population of 70,000.

Sir Stamford Raffles, who was Governor of Java during the short period of English occupation, was so impressed with the commercial importance of Batavia, that he persuaded the British Government, upon the cession of the island, to found a rival port on the opposite side of the Straits of Malacca. Singapore, the town due to this act of political foresight, is built upon a small island at the extremity of the Malay peninsula. Although it is almost exactly on the equator, it enjoys a more temperate climate than its older rival. It also possesses vastly superior accommodation for shipping. While Batavia, owing to the silting of the river already mentioned, is now some miles from the sea, Singapore possesses two commodious harbours, and has far outstripped the older town in commercial importance. There is a monument marking the spot where Lady Raffles was buried in the green glades of the gardens at Buitenzorg; but the statue of Sir Stamford Raffles looks forth to the sea from the centre of the broad grass-clad esplanade of Singapore.

Footnotes:

[9] "Not many years later (*i.e.* than 1602, the date of Wolfert's victory over the Portuguese Admiral Mendoza), at the distance of a dozen leagues from Bantam, a congenial swamp was fortunately discovered in a land whose volcanic peaks rose two miles in the air, and here a town duly laid out with canals and bridges, and trim gardens and stagnant pools, was baptized by the ancient and well-beloved name of Good Meadow, or Batavia, which it bears to this day" (Motley, "United Netherlands").

[10] Native carriage much like the sadoe, but never used by Europeans.

[11] I have taken this inscription as I found it translated in D'Almeida's "Life in Java," from which I have also abridged the story.

CHAPTER V.
THE HINDU TEMPLES.

The temple remains generally—The connection between Buddha and Brahma—The Boro-Boedoer—Loro-Jonggrang.

Of the temple ruins of Java, considered generally, Mr. Wallace says, "It will take most persons by surprise to learn that they far surpass those of Central America, perhaps even those of India."[12] Yet it is only recently that these great works have been recovered to the world. A Dutch engineer who was sent to construct a fort at Klaten, in 1797, found that a number of architectural remains existed in the neighbourhood of Brambanan, of which no account had been given. The natives, it appeared, regarded them as the work of some local deity, and, indeed, were in the habit of worshipping one conspicuous statue. He also found much difficulty in sufficiently clearing the ruins of the overgrowth of vegetation, so as to get an adequate view. Eventually he succeeded in making some rough sketches of them. In the year following the English occupation (1812), Colonel Colin MacKenzie visited Brambanan, and made an accurate survey of the ruins in that neighbourhood, which he sketched and described. At the instance of the Governor, Sir Stamford Raffles, Captain Butler was then sent to make drawings of the buildings, and to report upon them. This was the first methodical exploration of the Hindu ruins in Java; but it was only partial, and related almost exclusively to the Brambanan neighbourhood. A quarter of a century later, when the discovery of photography had made an exact reproduction of the sculptures possible, the Dutch Government instituted an exhaustive survey of the Boro-Boedoer temple. In July, 1845, M. Shaefer was commissioned to execute photographs of the bas-reliefs, but he was only partially successful. Two years later, an engineer, M. F. C. Wilsen, was sent out from Holland, and, after giving satisfactory proofs of his skill, definitely appointed in 1849, by a decree of the Council of Netherlands India, to make drawings of the bas-reliefs and statues of this temple. He was assisted by M. Schönburg Mulder. They commenced in April, 1849, and completed the whole of the task they had undertaken in the year 1853. M. Mulder's drawings proved, however, to be useless, and a new assistant, M. Mieling, was appointed. After various troubles, the drawings were finally completed in 1871, and the letterpress and plates published in 1874. This great literary work, consisting of several hundreds of large lithographed plans and drawings of sculptures and statues, with a complete account written by Dr. C. Leemans, director of the Public Museum at Leiden, was produced under the direction of the Dutch Minister of the Colonies. But even this splendid account of the Boro-Boedoer temple is not complete; since the date of its publication a new series of bas-reliefs have been discovered, and are being gradually photographed.

In connection with the temples of Brambanan and Kalasan, also, new and interesting discoveries are being made from year to year. Indeed, images and sculptured stones are continually found all over the island. At Gunong Praü, forty miles south-west of Samarang, and further east, at Kediri and in Malang, there are large tracts of ruins; but the most imposing and interesting for the traveller are to be found in the centre of the island, in the neighbourhood of Magalang and Djokja, in positions indicated by the accompanying map. I shall endeavour first to give the reader a general idea of the extent and nature of these remains, and then, after a few remarks on the connection between Buddha and Brahma, to describe more at length the Boro-Boedoer temple, and that of Loro-Jonggrang, near Brambanan, the former of which is Buddhistic, and the latter Brahmanic, or Saivite.

SKETCH MAP
OF
JAVA.

RAILWAYS
ROUTES BY ROAD
Note. Java is 630 Miles long by 120 to 50 Miles broad

At Boro-Boedoer, ten miles from Magalang, there are the remains of the vast temple of that name; and about a mile distant, on the nearer bank of the Prago river, is the small and externally insignificant temple of Mendoet. Inside this latter is a vaulted chamber, the roof of which springs from walls twenty feet in height, and rises to sixty feet in the centre, covering a fine statue of Buddha.

At Brambanan, a village near Djokja, there is a large mass of ruins, of which the most important are the temple of Loro-Jonggrang and a group of small temples called Tjandi Sewoe, or Thousand Temples. In the neighbourhood of the former ruins there are six large and fourteen small temples, twenty separate buildings in all. The ruins of the latter group cover a space of six hundred, square feet, and contain many splendid colossal figures. They are arranged in five regular parallelograms, consisting of an outer row of eighty-four temples, a second of seventy-six, a third of sixty-four, a fourth of forty-four, and a fifth (forming an inner-parallelogram) of twenty-eight. The centre is occupied by a large cruciform temple, ornamented with sculpture, and surrounded by flights of steps. All of these remains are greatly marred by the luxurious growths of tropical vegetation which cover them.

Half a mile further are the Tjandi Kali Bening, or Temples of Kalasan. Here there is a very fine and well-preserved temple, seventy-two square feet in extent, of which Mr. Wallace says that it is "covered with sculptures of Hindu mythology that surpass any that exist in India." There are also other ruins of palaces, halls, and temples in the neighbourhood.[13]

The stones used for the construction of the Boro-Boedoer and other temples in Java, and for the images found throughout the island, are of volcanic origin. They are supplied by the numerous volcanoes in the island, and carried down the sides of the mountains to the plains below in lava streams. To-day such stones are used largely for making roads. There is, however, a little limestone found in the southern districts of the island.

In the Boro-Boedoer, at Mendoet, and in the Tjandi Sewoe, Buddha was worshipped; but in the Temple of Loro-Jonggrang at Brambanan, and in the Temples of Kalasan, Siva (the third person of the Hindu Trinity—Brahma, Vishnu, Siva) was the central object of adoration. As the connection between the religion of Buddha and Brahma has been often misunderstood, a few words on this point may be of service to the reader.

Brahmanism, which was the established worship of the Hindus when Buddha taught, was a religion which admitted of many sects; and Buddha, although his ethical system was independent of Brahmanic theology, recognized the existence of the popular deities. The distinction, then, between Brahmanism and Buddhism is purely arbitrary; the latter is merely a new growth of the former, and they both exist in British India at the present day. In China also there is a similar fusion of religious beliefs, where there are three established cults—those of Brahma, Confucius, and of the Taöists, or nature-worshippers. The Confucian religion is rather a system of ethics than a cult; but the rites of the Buddhist and Taöist temples are attended indiscriminately by the majority of the Chinese, the priests of the separate temples alone confining themselves to the worship of a particular deity. In India, however, the special followers of the two systems do not exhibit an equal liberalism of sentiment; while the worship of Brahma is considered orthodox, the cult of Buddha is regarded as heretical. The Buddhistic temples of Java, coming midway between the oldest Buddhistic temples of India and the modern shrines in Burmah, Ceylon, and Nepaul, the present seats of the cult, supply an interesting *lacuna* in the antiquities of Buddhism. The Javan form of this religion is especially allied to that of Nepaul. It bears a general resemblance to the Buddhism of Northern India, but is distinct from that of

Ceylon and the south. It is not surprising, therefore, that ruins of temples dedicated to the services of both religions should exist side by side, nor that the grosser and more popular Brahmanic forms should have developed more largely than the more spiritual worship of Buddha, both in India to-day and in Java previously to the Mohammedan conquest.

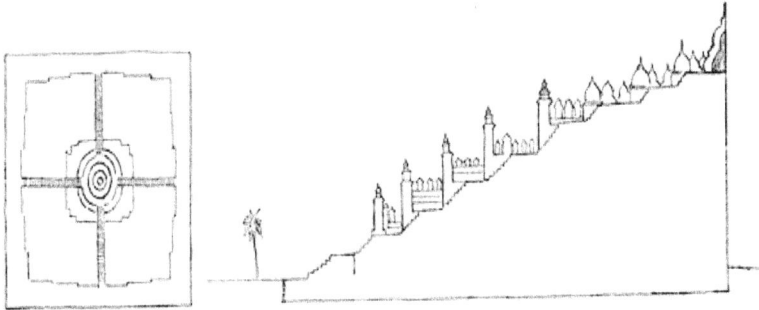

GROUND PLAN.

SECTION OF THE BORO-BOEDOER TEMPLE.

The temple of Boro-Boedoer is built upon a slight rounded eminence, the last of a chain of hills on the eastern bank of the river Prago. The entire edifice rests upon an equilateral base of six hundred and twenty feet, situated due N.S.E. and W., and rises gradually in terraces adapted in design to the form of the hill. These consist of two lower terraces which are square in form; four galleries (or passages, with sculptures on either side), which are still rectangular in form, but have twenty angles to admit of their following the rounded contour of the hill; and four terraces, of which the first has twelve angles, while the remaining three are circular, adorned with cupolas, each containing a statue of Buddha; and finally the whole is surmounted by a huge cupola, fifty feet in diameter, in which rests the central figure of Buddha. Access from one terrace to another is gained by four flights of steps, running up the centre of each front, at the several entrances of which are placed two huge lion-monsters. Dr. Leemans, in his account of the building, enumerates *five* galleries; but in reality there are only four, since the outside of what he calls the first gallery is merely a second basis for the whole structure, as is shown by the nature of its decoration, viz. simple architectural designs and groups of deities. The lower terrace, of which Dr. Leemans only guessed the existence, is now being excavated and photographed section by section. Only one section is kept open at any given time, because the earth is necessary to support the vast mass of stonework which forms the entire building, and it was for this reason, namely, to prevent the structure from breaking up, that this terrace was formerly banked up. It is found that this lower terrace is decorated with sculptures representing ordinary mundane scenes, the world being the basis on which all the higher religious phenomena rest. In the first gallery (Leemans' second), the bas-reliefs represent a continuous selection of scenes from the historical life of Buddha; in the second, there are sculptures of the lesser deities recognized in the Brahmanic worship, such deities having been adopted into the Buddhistic pantheon; in the third the higher deities are represented, where the *shrine*, and not the deity, is worshipped; in the fourth there are groups of Buddhas; and in the central dome there is the incomplete statue of the Highest Buddha—*Adibuddha*. This is unfinished by design, in order to indicate that the highest deity cannot be represented by human hands, having no bodily but only a spiritual existence.

"OM, AMITAYA! measure not with words
Th' Immeasurable; nor sink the string of thought
Into the Fathomless. Who asks doth err,
Who answers, errs. Say nought."

Such is the design of this great religious monument, of which even the bare ruins, in their melancholy magnificence, inspire the mind of the spectator with mingled feelings of wonder and solemnity.

The temple of Loro-Jonggrang is one in which, as at Kalasan, the object of worship was Siva, and not Buddha. This god, as already stated, was the third of the three persons of the Hindu Trinity; the first being Brahma, or the Creator, and the second Vishnu, the Preserver. Siva, the Destroyer, is also the Reproducer, and appears in Java to have been worshipped under three forms: (1) as Mahadeva, or the Great God; (2) as Mahayogi, or the Great Teacher; and (3) as Mahakala, or the Destroyer. Guru (or Goeroe) is an alternative name for Siva Mahayogi, and his statues in this temple are so called. The edifice is greatly inferior in size to that of Boro-Boedoer; it rests upon a rectangular basement having twelve angles, and measuring some eighty feet across in either direction. Like the former temple, its position is almost exactly square with the points of the compass. The basement is ornamented with ordinary religious ornaments, consisting of sacred trees and lions. Above this is a gallery, of which the parapet on the inner side is decorated with scenes taken from the Ramayana (the second of the two great Indian epics), while the opposite wall of the temple is adorned with forms of deities. In the centre or body of the temple are four chambers, one of which—the principal—is itself larger, and contains a larger image than the others. They are each alike approached by flights of steps in the centre of the four sides of the edifice. The deities represented are—in the northern chamber, Durga; in the western, Ganesa; and in both the southern and eastern, Guru. Now, according to the Brahmanic pantheon, Durga (*the* Goddess) was the mother, and Guru the father, of Ganesa, the elephant-headed God of Wisdom. The connection between Siva and the Rama epic is this. The Ramayana is the history of the incarnation of Vishnu as Rama, and contains an account of the war waged by Rama with the giant Ravana, the demon king of Ceylon. In the poem mention is made of the Vedic god Indra and his Maruts. Subsequently Siva, the world destroyer, was identified with Indra in the form of Rudra, the god of tempests; hence the appropriateness of scenes from this story on a Saivite temple. It only remains to add that the name of the temple, *Loro-Jonggrang*, is simply the native name given to the particular Durga (or Goddess of Efficient Virtue) represented in the shrine, and means literally the "Maiden with beautiful hips."

NOTE.—In view of the late appearance of the Adibuddha (probably the tenth century), I have thought it desirable to state that the theory of the general design of the Boro-Boedoer contained in the text is based upon a very interesting conversation which I had with M. Groeneveldt, who is a member of the Council of Netherlands India and Director of the Museum at Batavia. Professor Rhys Davids has pointed out an interesting distinction between the Boro-Boedoer and the Buddhist shrines in India, viz. that, whereas the cupolas at Boro-Boedoer are hollow, the *dagabas* of British India are always solid. In the Annex will be found a detailed account of the various routes and the cost, etc., of travelling from Batavia to the temple districts in the centre and east of Java.

Footnotes:

[12] "Malay Archipelago."

[13] For this general account of the ruins in the neighbourhood of Djokja I am indebted to the accounts of Raffles and Wallace.

ANNEX TO CHAPTER V.
THE ROUTES TO THE TEMPLES.

Supposing that the traveller has been landed at Batavia, and wishes to visit the ruins in the east of the island, he will have the choice of three routes. First, he may sail by a Netherlands India boat to Samarang (or Soerabaia, if, as often happens from December to February, it is impossible to land at the former place owing to the surf); this occupies about thirty-six hours. There is an excellent hotel at Samarang—the Pavilion—where the night can be spent, and the following day the train will carry him to Amberawa, a distance of 50 miles by rail (or 30 by road). Here the railway stops, and a carriage must be taken to Magalang, the next town (with splendid views of the two volcanoes, Merbaboe and Merapi), which is some 20 miles further on, and where a halt must be made for the night. Ten miles' driving will take him to the Boro-Boedoer; the drive is one of extraordinary beauty. After visiting the Boro-Boedoer and the neighbouring temple of Mendoet, it is usual to return by way of Djokja (25 miles), which is the centre of numerous ruins. If, however, it is intended to travel overland, there are two routes available. The first is the regular posting route along the northern coast; the second lies to the south, and is perhaps more interesting. If the regular route is chosen, the traveller will proceed by rail as far as Bandong, a distance of some 90 miles; and then drive to Cheribon (80 miles), a place on the northern coast; and then, following the coast-line, from Cheribon to Tegal (40 miles); from Tegal to Pekalongan (35 miles); and from Pekalongan to Samarang (68 miles). In all these places there are good hotels, but two horses, and in some places four (as in the last stage, where the road passes over mountains), would be necessary. Such a journey in a carriage would cost (apart from hotel expenses) £20, or, if it were done in a cart (sadoe) and two horses, half that sum.

If he pursues the second route, he will not leave the railway before Garoet. From Garoet he will proceed to Kalipoetjan (100 miles) by carriage; this occupies two days, and Manongyaya (with a hotel) is passed, and Bandar, where there is sleeping-accommodation to be had. From Kalipoetjan he will make his way to Tjilatjap by native canoe, crossing the Kinderzee, a large lagoon, in eight or nine hours, and passing some villages built on piles. There is also a curious cave and some edible swallow-nests to be seen. In travelling by this route it is necessary to take a servant to interpret with the natives. From Tjilatjap the railway runs to Djokja. This town is about 25 miles from the Boro-Boedoer temple; the road is bad, and at times covered with dust to the depth of a foot or more, so that three horses are necessary. Even then the journey occupies four or five hours, although it is quite possible to return on the same day. There is an inn at the small village near the temple, but it is not sufficiently inviting to merit more than a transitory visit; at the same time, there is nothing to prevent the gentlemen of the party from staying the night at Boro-Boedoer if they felt so inclined. From Djokja, of course, the railway extends to Samarang and to Soerabaia. Especially the town of Solo (or Soerakarta), which is the junction where the line branches north or east, is worthy of a visit, as being the best centre for seeing native ceremonies. In conclusion I append a table of distances, means of conveyance, and cost (this latter being approximate only as depending upon individuals).

NOTE.—The regular hotel charge all through Java is five or six florins a day (= 10s.). Twelve florins = £1.

FIRST ROUTE.

Places.	Means of Conveyance.	Cost.		Number of Miles.	Time.
Batavia to Samarang	Steamboat	60	florins	240	36 hours.
Samarang to Amberawa	Train	8	"	50	
Amberawa to Magalang —	Cart	10	"	— 20	
	Carriage	20	"		
Magalang to Boro-Boedoer —	Cart	5	"	— 10	
	Carriage	10	"		

SECOND ROUTE.

Places.	Means of Conveyance.	Cost.		Number of Miles.	Time.
Batavia to Bandong	Train	—	"	90	
Bandong to Cheribon —	Cart	30	"	— 80	10 "
	Carriage	60	"		

Cheribon to Tegal	—	Cart	15	"	—	40	4 "
		Carriage	50	"			
Tegal to Pekalongan	—	Cart	15	"	—	35	4 "
		Carriage	60	"			
Pekalongan to Samarang	—	Cart	30	"	—	50	11 "
		Carriage	70	"			

THIRD ROUTE.

Batavia to Garoet	Train	—	"	100	
Garoet to Kalipoetjan	Carriage	29	"	100	2 days.
Kalipoetjan to Tjilatjap	Native canoe	15	"	—	8 or 9 hrs.
Tjilatjap to Djokja	Train	—	"	90	

CHAPTER VI.
BUITENZORG.

Batavian heat—To Buitenzorg by rail—Buitenzorg— Kotta Batoe—
Buffalo—Sawah land—Sketching a Javan cottage.

Once in Java, and a visit to Buitenzorg is a matter of course. In the first place, Buitenzorg is to the Dutch possessions in the East what Simla is to British India; and, in the second, it possesses a strong attraction in its famous Botanical Gardens.

After a week of Batavia, the European or Australian traveller begins to want a change. It is not that there is at any time any extraordinary thermometrical heat to be encountered. It is simply that, not being an orchid, he finds it does not suit him to live in the warm damp atmosphere of a hothouse. What he suffers from most is the want of sleep. Probably he has not learnt to take two solid hours of sleep in the afternoon. He says to himself, "Pooh! this is nothing to the sun in India." He remembers that when he was in Australia the thermometer frequently registered 20° higher than it does here. It is all nonsense to call this a hot country, he thinks. So he hails a sadoe and drives off to the Kali Bezar to see the agent of his steamship company, when he ought to have been dressed in the luxurious freedom of pyjamas, and sleeping peacefully upon his great square bed, with the mosquito curtains securely drawn.

When night comes, the heat is apparently just as intense, and he lies awake, saying bad words about the mosquitoes which buzz around him, until the small hours of the morning. When his "boy" wakes him at six o'clock, he feels as if he had had no sleep at all. All the same it is a little cooler now; so he gets up to enjoy the fresh air outside in the verandah. After he has had his coffee and some bananas or a slice of pomelo, and taken his bath, he feels tolerably alive. This impression is heightened by a gallop over the King's Plain; and by the time he has had his breakfast he feels as "fit as anything." So he hardens his heart and does the same thing again to-day, except that, knowing the uselessness of trying to sleep before the temperature falls after midnight, he plays billiards at the club until he is turned out, and then spends the rest of the evening on a friend's verandah, seated in a long chair, consuming long drinks, and smoking long cigars.

It is not surprising, therefore, that the average globe-trotter finds a week of Batavia about enough at a time. He confides his emotions to his friend, who is a resident. This latter says, "Can't sleep? You should go to Buitenzorg; you'll sleep all night there." So he leaves his heavy luggage behind in the hotel, and packs a bag, jumps into a sadoe, and in less than two hours he finds himself in one of the healthiest climates in the world, and in the midst of surroundings as novel as they are delightful.

The train by which I had arranged to travel to Buitenzorg left the Weltevreden station at the convenient hour of half-past four in the afternoon. It only stopped once, and accomplished the distance in the fairly good time of one hour and twenty minutes. Here, again, as at Tanjong Priok, I was agreeably surprised with the size and convenience of the stations. The railway employés were Chinese and Javanese. The latter were dressed in peaked caps and blue serge coats and trousers, but wore rather unnecessarily waist-clothes and head-bands on the top of their European dress.

In Java, as elsewhere, the Anglo-Saxon abounded. The occupants of the railway carriage were, with two exceptions, English, like myself. There was a member of the Upper House of one of our colonial legislatures and his wife, the sister of a prominent English politician. With them I was already acquainted. But an English gentleman, who occupied one of the corner seats of the compartment, engaged in reading the *Field*, was a stranger.

The train passed by rice-fields, plantations of sugar cane, of bananas, and of Indian corn. On either side of us was a rich and highly cultivated country. There were hedgerows as neat as those which separate our English fields; and here and there a fox-hunter would have observed with disgust that barbed wire fences had spread as far as Java. At regular intervals, bamboo cottages with red-tiled roofs had been built for the signalmen. Among the fields were scattered groups of tropical trees, palms, and bamboos; and more than once we caught far-off glimpses of high mountains. The whole landscape was clothed in a supreme verdure.

As we approached the neighbourhood of Buitenzorg, the sky suddenly became overcast. Tremendous masses of dense black clouds rushed up from the horizon, throwing into relief the slopes of the mountains on which the sun was still shining brilliantly, and deepening the verdure of the rice-fields by their shadows. A few minutes of pelting rain and a flash or two of vivid lightning low down on the horizon, and once more the sky was clear and the landscape smiling and peaceful.

The town of Buitenzorg is situated on the slopes of the great volcanic mountain Salak, in 106° 53' 5" east longitude, and 6° 35' 8" south latitude. Although the elevation is only seven hundred feet above sea-level, the heat is never overpowering in the daytime, and the nights are delightfully cool. The mean temperature at noon, as indicated by the thermometer, is 82° Fahrenheit; but in the dry season as much as 88° is sometimes registered. Moreover while on an average there are five months of dry weather in Java and three in Batavia, three weeks without rain is considered unusual in Buitenzorg. The heat of the sun, therefore, is tempered by a rainfall which is not only very heavy, but very uniform; and when Batavia is steaming with moist heat, and the plains of the interior are scorched and dry, in Buitenzorg the gardens are still verdant and the air still tonic.

Besides Salak, which rises to a height of seven thousand feet, there is another and still loftier mountain mass in the immediate neighbourhood of the town. This is the double-peaked Pangerango and Gedé. All three mountains are volcanic. Salak, however, has been silent since the eruption of 1699, and the peak of Pangerango is an extinct volcanic cone; the only sign of activity is the light wreath of smoke which is generally to be seen hanging over the summit of Gedé. The slopes of these great mountains are clothed with a foliage which is kept perennially fresh by the abundant rains. Seen from rising ground, they enrich the landscape with the beauty of their graceful elevations; from the lower levels of the town, and in contrast to the foliage of palm or bamboo, their sheer height is manifested by the intense blueness of the background they afford.

Buitenzorg has long been the favourite resort of the officials and merchants of Batavia. In course of time the train service will no doubt be improved; as it is, busy men run down to see their families, or merely to enjoy the comparative coolness of the air for the "week end," or even for a single night.

The town itself contains a population of four thousand inhabitants. It has an excellent club, a museum, a race-course, and several good hotels. The summer residence of the Governor-General is in the centre of a large and beautifully wooded park, in which a number of deer are kept. It is an extensive building, consisting of an elevated central portion with wings on either side. It is built in the usual classical style affected by the Dutch for their public buildings, and is ornamented with pilasters and pediments. Part of the park is occupied by the famous Botanical Gardens, which form the supreme attraction of the place to the scientific visitor. The Governor-General, as the highest official in the Dutch East Indies, receives a salary of 160,000 florins a year. While this personage is at Buitenzorg he may be frequently observed driving down the great avenue of Kanarie trees in his state coach drawn by four horses. In close connection with the palace (as the Governor-General's residence is called), but at some distance from the town, large and convenient barracks have lately been completed for the better accommodation of the European troops.

I had been told not to omit to visit Batoe Toelis, "the place of the written stone," where there is an ancient inscription, and Kotta Batoe with its celebrated bath presided over by a Chinaman. My first expedition was to this latter place. There were three of us bent upon a swim before breakfast, and in order to save time we took a sadoe. The beauty and extent of the view increased as we ascended the slopes of Mount Salak. When we had driven some three miles we left the sadoe, with strict injunctions to the driver to wait till we returned, and proceeded to accomplish our quest on foot. There were three baths in all, natural basins of rock fed by streams of mountain water, and shaded by the dense foliage of lofty trees. One of them is circular in form, and the water is curiously coloured, by some trick of reflection or refraction, to a dull steely blue. A plunge in the clear cool water was well worth the trifling fee we paid to the celestial, and we returned to our hotel with a famous appetite for breakfast.

It was on the occasion of this drive that I first made the acquaintance of that useful domestic animal, the buffalo (*Bos Sondaicus*). He is a very "fine and large" animal of a mouse colour, with white legs and a patch of white on his quarters; and has long horns lying back on his neck, where they cannot be the slightest use to him. His Javan masters find him very docile, but he has an awkward way with strangers. He is generally to be found under the care of a small boy, who is seated on his broad back, and who touches him with a rod on this side or that according to the direction which he desires the animal to take. I have already described the simple but effective plough to which he is yoked when working the sawahs,[14] and the methods employed by the natives for the cultivation of rice.

From almost any elevated point it is possible to get views of the sawahs in the neighbourhood of Buitenzorg. The form and extent of the separate fields divided by the water-courses vary with the nature of the country. Each field is itself perfectly level, and is separated by as little as half a foot, or as much as four feet, from those immediately above and beneath it. The slopes of Gedé are covered with such a series of vast and irregular terraces. Seen from Buitenzorg the general effect is not unlike that of the tiers of a theatre, while in the distance the individual terraces show smooth surfaces varying in colour from emerald green to saffron yellow, or flashing with the brightness of still and sunlit waters.

Indeed, there is much to be seen at Buitenzorg with but little expenditure of time or trouble. Close at hand is the Campong, or Chinese town, with its quaint shops and busy market-place. Immediately beneath the hotel numberless bamboo cottages crowded with Javanese peasants can be found for the looking. They lie in the midst of groves of cocoanut palms, hidden away almost as completely as if they were a hundred miles instead of a hundred yards from the Belle Vue.

A JAVANESE COTTAGE.

I spent one whole morning sketching a cottage which I found within a stone's throw of the hotel. Without any ceremony, I walked into the midst of the family circle, and seated myself under the shelter of a wood shed. Had I known enough Malay, I should certainly have first asked permission before I ventured upon such an intrusion, for I have found a sketching-book an almost universal passport to civility. As it was, I assumed an air of conscious innocence, which I trusted would soon remove any awkward suspicions which might arise in the mind of the owner of the house, and proceeded to unpack my sketching-traps. I then quickly sketched in the group on the verandah, consisting of the mother and children. Before I had finished they all ran away in alarm, and for the next half-hour the front of the house was entirely deserted. I suppose they made up their minds at last that I was harmless, for they gradually came back and resumed their usual manner of life. The mother was occupied with keeping two small children in order. Besides these, there was a little boy and a girl. This latter was the oldest of the family. She was not so shy as her mother; on the contrary, she arranged herself in a most becoming attitude against the front of the verandah. Every now and then the mother showed her teeth and spoke crossly to the baby, and once when it cried she whipped it with a bit of palm-leaf until it came to a better mind—which it did promptly. After a time, a Chinaman called and had a talk with the lady of the house. I think he wanted a load of firewood. An old lady also came. I could not fathom *her* business, but, from the interest she manifested in the children, I expect she was a relative of the family.

About noon the father came back with a load of wood. He was a man of the world, and knew all about the performance. After he had looked at the sketch, the children, and finally the mother, all came round my stool and had a good long look at my work. Even so the mother would not let the children dab their toes into my paints, or generally become a nuisance. For this unexpected manifestation of a sense of the fitness of things, I felt grateful to her, and, before I went away, found a way of recompensing the children for the sorrow they must have felt at being compelled to relinquish such a rare opportunity for getting into mischief.

Every morning I found some quaint figure with which to enrich my sketch-book—a sarong-weaver, or a beggar crouching by the wayside, or a Hadji, with his large umbrella and green turban, the latter marking the fact of his having accomplished a pilgrimage to Mecca. But, interesting as were these human studies, my pleasantest recollections of Buitenzorg centre in the visit which I paid to the Botanical Gardens, under the guidance of the curator, Dr. Treub.

My account of this, however, and of the gardens generally, I reserve for the next chapter.

NATIVES SQUATTING.

CHAPTER VII.
THE BOTANICAL GARDENS.

History of the Buitenzorg gardens—Teysmann— Scheffer—Three separate branches—Horticultural garden—Mountain garden—Botanical garden— Dr. Treub—Lady Raffles' monument—Pandanus with aërial roots—Cyrtostachys renda—Stelecho-karpus— Urostigma—Brazilian palms—Laboratories and offices—Number of men employed—Scientific strangers.

Among the twenty or thirty tropical gardens established in the colonial possessions of the various European Powers, three stand pre-eminent—those of Calcutta, the Peradenia Gardens in Ceylon, and the Dutch gardens at Buitenzorg. It is only natural that a people so distinguished for horticulture as the Dutch should have turned to account the floral wealth of the Malay Archipelago, perhaps the richest botanical hunting-ground in the world. The Buitenzorg gardens, however, owe their present celebrity more to individual energy than to Government patronage.

Originally established in 1819, in a corner of the park surrounding the residence of the Governor-General, the exigencies of colonial finance subsequently required the withdrawal of almost all the provision originally made, and only a sum sufficient to support a single European gardener was left. The salary of this single official was taken from the funds appropriated to the maintenance of the park. It was to this post that J. E. Teysmann was appointed in 1830. Educated at one of the primary schools in Holland, and originally employed as an under-gardener, he had in that capacity accompanied Governor Van den Bosch to Java. Like our own Moffat (also an under-gardener), Teysmann rose by his energy and devotion to "great honour," and, half a century later, received a remarkable proof of the esteem in which he was held in the scientific world, consisting of an album, within which were inscribed the signatures of the donors—one hundred famous naturalists, ranging from Darwen to Candolle, the Genevan. It bore the inscription—

"Celeberrimo indefessoque J. E. Teysmann cum dimidium per sæculum Archipelagi indici thesaurum botanicum exploravit, mirantes collegæ."

During the period that the gardens ceased to exist as an independent institution—1830 to 1868—Teysmann continued to search throughout the islands of the Archipelago for rare and undiscovered plants with which to enrich them. He also published catalogues embodying the discoveries he had made, and finally arranged the plants and trees upon an excellent system, in which they are grouped in accordance with their natural relationships.

In 1868 the gardens once more became a public institution, with a curator and a recognized revenue. The new curator was Dr. Scheffer, of Utrecht, who in 1876 founded, in addition to the botanical gardens, a school of agriculture with a garden attached to it. This useful institution was subsequently suppressed by the Government, but the garden still survives alongside its parent at Buitenzorg. Dr. Scheffer died in 1880, when only thirty-six years of age. He was succeeded by the present curator, Dr. Treub.

The Dutch Government gardens in Java, known to the scientific world as the *Hortus Bogoriensis*,[15] and to the official as the *Nederlands Plantentuin te Buitenzorg*, contain three separate branches—the botanical gardens, a horticultural garden, and a mountain garden. Of these, the last is situated at some distance from the town, on the slopes of Mount Gedé. It occupies seventy-five acres of land at an altitude of between 4000 and 5000 feet, and is provided with a staff of ten natives working under a European gardener. I was told that, while all European, Australian, and Japanese flowers would grow there, it was found impossible to cultivate the fruits of such temperate regions, owing to the difficulty experienced in securing the necessary period of rest. I have since heard that in Fiji the difficulty is overcome by exposing the roots for some months, and thus preventing the sap from rising. Why not adopt this method in Java?

The horticultural garden adjoins the botanical gardens, and occupies forty acres. As already mentioned, it owes its existence to Dr. Scheffer, and it is, of course, devoted to strictly practical objects. Consequently, everything is arranged in such a manner as to make the most of the space. All the paths are at right angles or parallel to each other, and the garden generally is laid out with monotonous regularity. Yet no small part of the success of the Government gardens as an institution depends upon the produce of this department. It has for many years enabled the Government to distribute gratuitously the seeds and plants required for various colonial enterprises. Within its trim beds are contained tea and coffee plants, sugar-canes, caoutchouc and gutta-percha trees, *Erythroxylon coca* for cocaine, and trees producing tannin and oils. Various medicinal plants are also to be found here, and such as afford useful nourishment for cattle. The necessary labour for this garden is supplied by a head-gardener and seventy natives.

The botanical gardens occupy ninety acres of the southern corner of the park, which itself forms their northern limit. On the east they are bounded by the river Tjiliwong, and on the west and south by the high-road from Batavia. Through the centre there runs the famous *Allée des Kanaries* (*Canarium commune*), the boughs of which form an arched roof one hundred feet from the ground. Leading right and left from this central avenue run other smaller avenues, roads, and paths, conducting to the different plots in which the various families of plants are contained, in accordance with the system of arrangement introduced by Teysmann. Some of these paths, especially those leading to the lower level by the river-bank, are paved with pebbles after the manner of the "cobbled" streets of our English villages. To this Mr. Wallace, in his "Malay Archipelago," takes exception on the score of discomfort. I was assured, however, that they are a necessary evil, and that the heavy rains to which Buitenzorg was liable, made it necessary to have the firmest kind of pathway in such places. At either end of the avenue there are lodges, but no gates, and the gardens are left open day and night without any fear of injury. This fortunate condition of affairs is not unusual in Java, but in this case security is partly ensured by the proximity of a large military force and the frequent presence of the Governor-General.

As Dr. Treub had kindly offered to act as my guide, I found my way one morning to his house at the early hour of half-past seven. The residence provided for the curator is situated on the left side of the southern entrance. The deep verandah is furnished with some brilliant groups of flowers. Opening on to it is a little morning-room hung with some elegant engravings—reproductions of *Salon* pictures. Here I found Dr. Treub waiting for me.

After a few moments' conversation we left the house and passed down the avenue. Some hundred yards onwards, to the right, there is a stone monument interesting to Englishmen. It consists of a circular roof supported by pillars, protecting a funereal urn placed upon a square pedestal. On the pedestal the following inscription is engraved:—

"Sacred to the memory of Olivia Mariamne, wife of Thomas Stamford Raffles, Lieutenant-Governor of Java and its dependencies, who died at Buitenzorg on the 26th of November, 1814."

Although the site of this monument is more humble than that of Sir Thomas Raffles' statue at Singapore, it is scarcely less interesting; and the repair and preservation of the stonework is secured by a special clause in the treaty of cession. I think it was just here that Dr. Treub turned away from the Canary Avenue, and, taking one of the paths to the right, led me forward towards the river.

I had asked him if he would point out any trees specially worthy of being sketched, and he had very readily acceded to my request. After we had walked a few minutes, however, he said—

"I am in a difficulty; I do not know what to show you. We have some most curious plants in the garden, but there is nothing remarkable about them externally. I suppose you want something with a *cachet* for the public?"

I said he was quite right in his supposition. What I wanted was something of interest from a picturesque point of view to the general public.

"There," he said, pointing to a tall tree with a growth and foliage of no distinct character, "is a strychnine tree; from the berries of that tree we get nux vomica; but if you drew that, they would say, 'Why, it is an apple-tree; it is not worth going to the tropics to see that.'"

By this time we had almost reached the banks of the Tjiliwong, and again turning to the right, where grew the pandans, "There," he said, "is a tree with aërial roots. It comes from the Nicobar Islands, just north-west of Sumatra. I think it is about twenty-eight feet in height. No, the roots do not contribute to its nourishment; they are useless but very curious." From the pandans we passed to the palms. First we noticed a specimen of comparatively low growth, with its leaves springing from the ground like the leaves of a primrose—*Ladoicea Sechellarum*. It bore, I was told, the largest fruit and the largest leaves of any known tree, the former being two, and the latter ten, feet in diameter. "Unfortunately, there is no fruit on it," said Dr. Treub, "but you can see *that* in any museum. You see, the stems of the leaves are as hard as iron." Indeed, they gave quite a metallic ring as he drove the ferrule of his walking stick against them. A few steps further brought us to a tree which Dr. Treub said had no special characteristics, but was a perfect natural specimen of the palm family. It stood about forty feet in height, and was furnished with foliage which hung gracefully suspended from a straight tapering stem. Then at the next corner, where its beauty showed to advantage, we came upon a group of red-stemmed palms from the little island of Banka. A fortnight later I was anchored off Mentok, the capital of that island, in a Dutch mail boat; but at this time I had no knowledge of the *habitat* of this fair tree—nor, indeed, had I seen it before, although a few weeks afterwards I found two fine specimens growing on either side of the entrance of a private house at Singapore. It needs an expert to describe so rare a combination of brilliant colours and graceful form. Mr. Forbes, the naturalist, in his account of his "Wanderings in the Eastern Archipelago," tells how he passed down through "plots of amaryllideæ, iris, and other water-loving plants" in this quarter of the garden; and how he found the "glory" of "the richest *palmetum* in the world—the *Cyrtostachys renda*, whose long bright scarlet leaf-sheaths and flower-spathes, and its red fruit and deep yellow inflorescence hanging side by side, at once arrest the eye."

From this point we again ascended to the higher level of the garden by a path paved with pebbles and cut into steps. Then "faring on our way," we reached the division marked *Anonaceæ*, and there my eye came upon a sight which rivalled in wonder the golden bough of the sixth Æneid which the doves of Venus showed to Æneas:

"Tollunt se celeres, liquidumque per aëra lapsæ,
Sedibus optatis geminæ super arbore sidunt,
Discolor unde auri per ramos aura refulsit."

In this case the "contrasting golden beam" shone not from the foliage, but, stranger still, from the black trunk of a tall tree. It was a *stelecho-karpus*, or stem-flowering tree. The trunk from which the deep saffron flowers sprang was about one foot and three inches in diameter, and the flowers themselves were much like bunches of primroses, only darker in colour and divested of their leaves. Unlike Æneas, we passed forward without any floral spoils—for, indeed, we had no such awkward personage as Charon to reckon with— among dark, cool, tree-arched avenues of figs and banyans to the northern limit. On our way we paused once to notice a fine "sacred fig" of India (*urostigma*), a tree with remarkably angular boughs; and again when Dr. Treub stopped, and, pointing to the frangipane blossom, said, "That is the flower of religion in India, being sacred to Buddha; the Malays here call it the 'flower of the dead.'" In this quarter the trees were larger and of more robust growth, and the appearance of the garden more natural to my Northern eyes. A sudden turn brought us to a projecting spur, on which was built a little summer-house commanding a view of the surrounding country. Far away the double mountain Pangerango and Gedé rose blue and shadowy, with just a wreath of smoke showing from the volcanic peak. In the middle ground stretched masses of tropical forests edging the bright green terraces of the savah land. At our feet the river ran bubbling and fretting over the brown stones.

In returning we skirted the central lake, and, having crossed the avenue, passed down a broad roadway lined with rich foliage. This was so arranged as to afford a view of Mount Salak to the southern windows of the Governor-General's residence. It was one of the many glimpses which appeared of a sheer height of dark azure contrasted with the bright green of palm or bamboo. Leaving this, we passed down an avenue of Brazilian palms, running parallel to the Canary Avenue. Each tree was almost too faultlessly perfect in its graceful foliage and smooth rounded stem, and of apparently equal height. Round the surfaces of these stems the green leaves and purple flowers of convolvuli clung. A few yards beyond the termination of this avenue we left the path and entered a wilderness of climbing plants. Carefully advancing (for there were arms stretched out on every side ready to pluck flesh or clothing), we took our stand opposite the coils of a huge climbing palm.

"There are branches," said Dr. Treub, "from this plant six hundred feet in length; it passes, as you see, from tree to tree."

On reaching the path, I found that we had completed the circuit of the gardens, and were once more in the neighbourhood of the nurseries and buildings. These latter are numerous and extensive, for the curator of the Buitenzorg gardens aims not only at obtaining a wide range of vegetable products, and thus serving the needs of colonial industries, but also at accomplishing researches in the pathology and physiology of plants. In this way Dr. Treub expects a useful development for the tropical gardens generally, which he considers have only lately become genuine centres of scientific research. At Buitenzorg, in addition to a museum containing an extensive herbarium and a botanical library of over five thousand volumes, there are numerous laboratories and offices accommodating the curator and his three assistants, and draughtsmen, who are competent to employ the methods of photography and lithography in reproducing the forms of plants. Under the direction of this staff there are employed a number of natives, including three Malays with special botanical knowledge, a head-gardener, and nine under-gardeners, and scarcely less than a hundred coolies. Altogether there are nine thousand distinct species of plants contained in the gardens. On our way to the strangers' laboratory we passed a number of trellis-work houses, with creepers trained over their sides and roofs. "You see," said Dr. Treub, with a smile, "we have *cool* houses here instead of *hot* houses. They are for forest plants accustomed to coolness and shelter."

I was especially asked to notice the completeness of the arrangements made for scientific visitors. The laboratory is seventy-five feet in length, and opposite each of the ten windows (five on either side) is placed a table fitted with optical instruments and other necessary means of botanical research. It is also provided with a small library and herbarium. In reference to the strangers' laboratory, Dr. Treub remarked that he specially desired to see Englishmen avail themselves of it. German and French *savants* had come to Buitenzorg to study, but no Englishmen as yet.

I visited these gardens on several occasions during my short stay at Buitenzorg, and often wandered among the dark tree-arched paths and avenues. On each occasion I found some new beauty. One day it was a lakelet covered with great water-plants; another day a gorgeous plot of orchids, or a fresh piece of landscape. These subsequent visits, however, lacked that which gave so great a charm to my first walk through the gardens—the spontaneous courtesy and graceful learning of the curator.

A HAPPY CELESTIAL.

Footnotes:

[15] *Bogor* is the native name for this place; *Buitenzorg* means "beyond care," and is therefore the equivalent of the French *sans sourci*.

CHAPTER VIII.
FROM BUITENZORG TO TJI WANGI.

View of Mount Salak—Railway travelling in Java— Soekaboemi—No coolies—A long walk—Making a *pikulan*—Forest path—Tji Wangi at last.

It is two in the afternoon, and I have just taken the curious Javan meal called *rice-table*. Everyone else in the hotel, visitors and servants alike, are asleep. The doors of my rooms are all open, and there is a through draught from the courtyard to the verandah, where I am seated in a long easy chair with arms extending at will after the manner of the tropics. By my side on a table are placed cigars, a glass of iced claret and water, and a novel.

The view from the back rooms of the Hôtel Belle Vue at Buitenzorg is famous. This afternoon I am looking at it for the last time, and it seems more wonderful than ever. Let me try to describe it.

Immediately in front is the great triangular mass of Mount Salak. The peak is 7000 feet above sea-level, and, like most of the Javan mountains, it rises to its full height almost clear from its base. The lower levels are luxuriantly covered with tropical forests, a covering which gradually thins and dwindles until the apex of the triangle stands out sharply against the sky. Between the hotel and the mountain there stretches a sea of waving treetops. In the distance it is deep blue; as it approaches it grows more and more green; then separate forms of palms and bamboos can be distinguished, with red-tiled or brown-thatched roofs showing between them. Immediately beneath me is the brown river Tjiliwong, with bamboo cottages on its banks and natives bathing in its waters.

Inside the courtyard no one is stirring. The dreamy silence is only broken by the voices that rise from the river below, by the clacking of the sarong weaver's shuttle or the dull boom of a far-away tom-tom.

Under such circumstances the conditions necessary for perfect physical enjoyment are very fully realized. Yet it is at such moments that one is apt to reflect how unimportant are these material considerations compared with the advantages of strenuous and reasoned action. One longs for the stir of life as it is felt in the great centres of European population;

"Better fifty years of Europe than a cycle of Cathay."

Well, I was going to see some European energy on the morrow. At Batavia an English resident had said, "When you are at Buitenzorg you should go on to Soekaboemi and see a coffee plantation.' Subsequently he wrote that his friend H—— would expect me on Tuesday at his coffee plantation with an unpronounceable name in the Preanger district. The morrow was Tuesday.

Soekaboemi was only thirty or forty miles away, but I left Buitenzorg at eight o'clock in order to escape the discomfort of travelling in the middle of the day. It goes without saying that trains in the tropics do not carry you along as quickly as the Flying Dutchman or the Scotch express. But I found the carriages comfortable enough, being built in the American fashion, and furnished with Venetians to keep out the sun and let in the air. Except the station-masters, all the officials were Chinese or Javan natives. The guard who looked at my ticket wore the traditional peaked cap and cloth uniform, but over his European garments he had appended as usual his airy native costume. Of the four classes of carriages two are reserved for Europeans, one for Chinese, and one for the natives.

In leaving Buitenzorg I made the mistake of taking a first-class ticket. In the first place, the carriage had not been dusted, and a cooly came in and disturbed me with his brush. He made such a cloud of dust that I had to beat a retreat. On my return I found the carriage clean, but the dust transferred to my baggage. In the next place, all the Dutch officials, and the planters and their wives, were travelling second class, and I was left to enjoy (?) my compartment in solitary grandeur. Had there been any one in the carriage, I should have found out that Soekaboemi was not the right station for H—— 's plantation. As it was I could open and shut windows at will, and I was free to make the best of my opportunities for sight-seeing—an object towards which the slow pace of the train and the frequent and lengthy stoppages materially contributed. Indeed, the crowds of natives at the stations were as well worth studying as the mountains and plantations. I never saw elsewhere, even in Java, such rainbow mixtures of colours as they contrived to bring into their cotton jackets and dresses; and as for their plaited hats, there was every possible variety of shape and size, from an umbrella to a funnel.

For the first few miles the line ran southwards between Salak and Gedé. On either side I could see stretches of mountain slopes luxuriously wooded, while the brown stream Tji Sadanie, a tributary of the Kali Besar, or "great river" of Batavia, playing hide-and-seek with the railroad, afforded more than one charming "bit" of river, tree, and mountain.

As we get away from the mountains the view widens. Masses of palms, dark green bamboos, and other tropical growths fill up the distance. In the foreground are irrigated rice terraces, with gleaming waters and the freshest of verdure. Here copper-coloured natives are at work. Men are ploughing the wet soil of the sawahs with buffaloes; women—often with their babies slung on their backs with their long scarfs—are hoeing, or weeding, or reaping. As the average monthly temperature does not vary more than two degrees all the year round in Java, the process of preparing the ground, sowing, and reaping go on simultaneously in the ricefields. Every now and then we come across a queer little Noah's-ark cottage in the midst of bananas and bamboos, with a tall palm or two waving overhead. Salak remains long in sight. At first it towered in its pride of greatness, then it grew soft in the blue distance. At last the railway turns abruptly at Karan Tenjak, and it is gone.

As the train nears Soekaboemi the character of the country changes. Plantations of sugar in the level country and of tea on the uplands take the place of ricefields. The name Soekaboemi means "pleasant place," and the town is the centre of the planting interest in Java. In its immediate neighbourhood are coffee, cinchona, and tea plantations.

At a quarter to eleven the train drew up in a large and excellently arranged station. I at once made my way outside. Here I looked in vain for the horses and coolies I expected to meet me. After waiting some moments, I confided my troubles to a bystander, addressing him in French, which is spoken by the Europeans in Java almost as much as Dutch. Fortunately Tji Wangi—the unpronounceable name of H——'s plantation—seemed to be well known, and he grasped the situation at once.

"You ought to have gone to Tji Reingass," he said; "the coolies will be there."

"How far am I from Tji Wangi? Is it within driving distance?" I inquired.

"Yes."

"Can I take a sadoe?"

"Yes, certainly."

There were several sadoes outside the station at Soekaboemi. As my knowledge of Malay, the recognized language for communication between natives and Europeans, was strictly limited, I asked my new friend to find out if the Malay "boy" knew where Tji Wangi was. This he readily did, and told me that it was all right; that he would take me to Tji Wangi. So I got into the sadoe, expecting to be driven promptly to my destination.

But the thing was not so simple. After an hour and a half of driving over mountain roads, the Malay pulled up suddenly under the shelter of a wayside inn. While I was wondering why he stopped, he coolly took out my luggage and planted it in the middle of the road in front of the sadoe. After this very broad hint, I got out too.

"Mana Tji Wangi" ("Where is Tji Wangi")? I said.

For answer he pointed with his thumb over his shoulder to the mountain.

"Brapa lama" ("How long")?

"Suku jam" ("A quarter of an hour"), was the mendacious and unhesitating reply.

Meanwhile a cooly, who had been summoned from the ricefields, appeared upon the scene and took up my Gladstone bag. Nothing remained for me but to pay my mendacious Malay half the number of florins he demanded and follow my new guide.

As a matter of fact, Tji Wangi was ten miles away on the other side of the Goenoeng Malang, or Cross Mountain. This, of course, I did not know, and so I set off cheerfully up the side of the mountain. Although it was midday, the heat was not oppressive at this altitude (two thousand feet), and I was clothed for the tropics. When an hour had passed and there were still no signs of the plantation, I began to feel less cheerful. I stopped and interrogated the cooly. He smiled blandly. *He* at least was suffering from no misgivings. Like the young man in "Excelsior," he pointed upwards. We met some natives; I accosted them with "Mana Tji Wangi?" They too pointed up the mountain. At any rate, we were travelling in the right direction. I noticed that the natives we met behaved very differently from the saucy sadoe-drivers in the towns. As we passed they stood on one side with their heads uncovered. When I spoke to them, they squatted down and sat with their legs tucked up under them and their hats off in a most uncomfortable way. I afterwards learnt that these traditions of Oriental etiquette were preserved by the Dutch and English planters in the interests of discipline. As the plantations are often long distances apart, the Europeans have to rely upon moral force to maintain their ascendency. Another half-hour passed and still no signs of Tji Wangi. We had met no Europeans, and I was beginning to get uneasy, when we came to a second inn.

Here I ordered a halt. The shade of the projecting roof was very welcome. My eyes could not reach the dark interior, but they ranged hungrily—I had eaten nothing since my early breakfast—over the edibles laid out in front. There were fruits and cakes, little messes of vegetables, dried fish, and other odd-looking delicacies on plates. I decided on a big bunch of bananas. In payment I gave a half-florin—worth rather less than a shilling of English money—and I received in return quite a handful of silver and copper coins. I concluded that bananas were not expensive in Java.

While I was eating my bananas, my cooly set to work to make a *pikulan*, or shoulder-piece. He took a long bamboo and stripped off the leaves and branches with his *gaulok*, a long knife which every native carries at his waist. By the aid of this contrivance—borrowed from China—the Javan natives carry burdens up to half a hundredweight without apparent exertion for long distances. The spring of the bamboo eases the pressure on the shoulder. On the same principle, an Australian carries his swag with a lurch forward.

While he was busied with the pikulan, the cooly talked over the affairs of the *Tuan Ingris* (English gentleman) to a crowd of natives. Suddenly I heard the word *kuda*. Fortunately *kuda* (horse) was one of the words I knew: and I at once ordered the kuda to be brought. Half a dozen natives set off to find it. It turned out to be a very diminutive pony, but I was not prepared to criticize.

We set out from the inn under brighter auspices. The cooly slung my Gladstone bag at one end of the pikulan, and another small bag, with a big stone to balance, at the other. He moved with an elastic step, as if there was no greater pleasure in the world than carrying bags up mountain paths, and beat the kuda hands down.

Relieved of the fatigue of walking, I could admire the mountain scenery. As we climbed higher and higher, the stretches of green country grew more extensive, and the blue mountains seemed to grow loftier in the distance. Once over the saddle of the mountain, we descended rapidly into a region of almost virgin forest. Ferns and large-leaved trees overhung the path; from the verdant undergrowth there sprang at intervals the vast round trunks of the rosamala trees. In the branches high above, and beyond the range of any gun, the wild pigeons fluttered and cooed. The spaces between the great trees were filled by a background of dense forest.

About five o'clock the red roofs of the plantation came in sight. In another five minutes I was being-welcomed with Anglo-Saxon heartiness. "Ah!" said H——, as he looked at my little pony. "I sent you down a horse that would have brought you up within the hour. You should have gone to Tji Reingass; that is our station, not Soekaboemi. Johnston ought to have known. Come in."

In H——'s comfortable den I soon forgot the various *contretemps* of my journey to Tji Wangi.

CHAPTER IX.
THE CULTURE SYSTEM.

Financial system previous to the British occupation— Raffles' changes—
Return of the Dutch—Financial policy—Van den Bosch Governor-
General—Introduction of the culture system—Its application to sugar—To
other industries—Financial results of the system— Its abandonment—
Reasons of this—Present condition of trade in Java—Financial outlook.

As I have already mentioned, the Colonial Government succeeded the Dutch
East India Company in the administration of Java towards the end of the last
century. During the period antecedent to the British occupation, the revenue
of the Government was derived from two monopolies: (1) that of producing
the more valuable crops, and (2) that of trading in all products whatever.
Meanwhile the mass of the natives were left entirely to the mercy of the
native princes, by whom they were subjected to all manner of exactions.

The financial results of this state of things were seen in the fact that in 1810
the gross revenue of Java was only three and a half million florins,[16] a sum
wholly inadequate to the requirements of administration.

During the five years of British occupation (1811-1816) Sir Stamford Raffles
was Lieutenant-Governor. He at once introduced reforms. The native
princes were displaced; the village community, with its common property
and patriarchal government, was modified; a system of criminal and civil
justice, similar to that in force in India, in which a European judge sat with
native assessors, was introduced; the peasants were given proprietary rights
in the soil they cultivated; and complete political and commercial liberty was
established. An inquiry into the nature of the respective rights in the soil of
the cultivator, the native princes, and the Government resulted in
establishing the fact that, of the subject territory the Government was sole
owner of seven-tenths. Of the remainder, two-tenths belonged to the
Preanger Regents, and one-tenth was occupied by private estates, chiefly in
the neighbourhood of Buitenzorg and Batavia. In order to teach the native
the western virtues of industry and independence, Raffles determined to
introduce the Ryotwarree system. The property in the land vested in the
Government was handed over to individual peasant proprietors. In return
for his land each proprietor was made individually and personally responsible
for the payment of his land tax, and his land was liable to be sold in
satisfaction of his public or private debts.

Before the English administration the peasant had paid—(1) a land rent for
his rice lands to the native princes, amounting to a sum equivalent to one-
half of the produce of sawah (irrigated) and one-third of tegal (unirrigated)
lands; and (2) a tax of forced labour to the Dutch Government, which took

the form of unpaid labour in the cultivation of the produce for export. Raffles abolished both, and in place of them he established a fixed money payment equivalent to a much smaller proportion of the produce of the land than had been paid before to the native princes alone.

The Dutch regained their East Indian possessions by the Treaty of London. On their return to Java, they restored the village community with its joint ownership and joint liability, and abolished all proprietary rights of the natives in the soil, only allowing ownership of land to Europeans. They contend that this attempt of Raffles to apply Western principles to an Eastern society had already proved disastrous. The peasants, on the one hand, had not acquired the habits necessary for the successful development of their holdings, but, on the other, through their inability to pay the land rent, were becoming hopelessly involved in debt to the Chinese and Arab money-lenders. The broad fact, however, remains that during the short period of British rule the revenue rose from three and a half to seven and a half million florins, and the population from four to five and a half millions.

As the old monopolies from which the chief part of the revenue had formerly been derived had been abolished by the policy of unrestricted commerce introduced by Raffles, it was necessary to find some other method of raising money. It was decided to retain the land tax as a basis of revenue, but, in order to make it more profitable, a return was made to the original principle of land tenure under native rule, by which the cultivator paid one-fifth of his labour and one-fifth of his produce in return for the usufruct of the land. One day of gratuitous labour in seven (the European week) was substituted for one day in five formerly given to the landlord. In certain districts, namely, those of which the Dutch became possessed by treaty and not by conquest, this contribution in kind and labour was paid to the native princes, and not to the Government. On private estates, again, as the Government had parted with their feudal rights in alienating the property, a tax of three-fourths per cent, on the estimated value of the property was substituted. This tax, called *verponding*, was at most equivalent to one-fifth of the net yearly income.

As before, the produce due from the peasants cultivating Government lands was commuted into a money payment assessed upon the rice crops; but this payment was made, not by the individual peasants, but by the *wedanas*, or village chiefs, on behalf of the whole community. Beside the land tax, an additional source of income remained in the profit arising from the sale of coffee, grown either by the Preanger Regents and sold to the Government at prices fixed by treaty, or on the coffee plantations established by Marshall Daendels, which were now restored.

These two methods of raising revenue were resorted to by the Dutch upon their return to the island, and continued in force during the period 1816-

1833. They were wholly inadequate. Whether the Dutch were right or not in characterizing Raffles' reforms as a failure, it is certain that nothing could be more desperate than the state of the island in the years immediately preceding the introduction of the culture system. At the end of the period 1816-1833 both revenue and population seem to have become stationary. The mass of the natives were becoming so impoverished that they ceased to be able to keep a supply of domestic animals and implements necessary for the cultivation of their lands. Apart from the princes, there was no class, merchants or tradespeople, possessing any wealth that could be taxed. Not only was the revenue stagnant, but, owing to a war with the sultans of the interior, a debt of over 35,000,000 florins was incurred by the Government. In a word, the colony seemed likely to become an intolerable burden to Holland. It was at this crisis that General Van den Bosch proposed the culture system as a means of rescuing the island from its financial and social difficulties.

The immediate object of the culture system was to extend the cultivation of sugar, coffee, and other produce suited for European consumption; its ultimate object was to develop the resources of the island. This latter was, of course, the most important. Van den Bosch saw that the natives would never be able to do this by themselves. In the first place, they were still organized on the patriarchal model in village communities; and, in the second, owing to the tropical climate and the extreme ease with which life could be sustained in so fertile a country, they were naturally indolent and unprogressive. He therefore proposed to organize their labour under European supervision. By this method he thought that he would be able both to raise the revenue and to improve the condition of the peasants by teaching them to grow valuable produce in addition to the rice crops on which they depended for subsistence. Van den Bosch became Governor-General of Java and its dependencies in 1830. Before leaving Holland he had made his proposals known, and obtained the approval of the Netherlands Government. He took with him newly appointed officials free from colonial traditions, and his reforms inspired such confidence, that a number of well-educated and intelligent persons were willing to emigrate with their families to Java in order to take up the business of manufacturing the produce grown under the new system. Upon his arrival in the island, a special branch cf the Colonial Administration was created. The first work of the new department was to found the sugar industry. It was necessary to supply the manufacturers with both capital and income. Accordingly, a sum amounting to £14,000 was placed to the credit of each manufacturer in the books of the department. Of this sum he was allowed to draw up to £125 per month for the expenses of himself and his family during the first two years. From the third year onwards he paid back one-tenth annually. Thus at the end of twelve years the capital was repaid. The manufacturer was to apply the capital so advanced to the construction of the sugar-mill, which was to be fitted with the best European machinery, and worked by water-power. Free labour, and timber from the Government plantations, was supplied; and the customs duties upon the machinery and implements imported were remitted. The building of the mills was supervised by the *contrôleurs*, the officials of the new department, and had to be carried out to their satisfaction. The department also undertook to see that the peasants in the neighbourhood of each mill should have from seven hundred to a thousand acres planted with sugar-canes by the time the mills were in working order. In Java, as in other Eastern countries, the landlord has the right of selecting the crop which the tenant is to plant, and therefore the peasants saw nothing unusual in this action of the Government. The contrôleurs ascertained, in the case of each village, how much rice land was necessary for the subsistence of the village, and they then ordered the remainder, usually one-fifth, to be planted with sugar-canes. At the same time, they explained that the value of the crop of sugar would be much greater than that of the rice crop, and promised that the peasants should be paid not only for the crops, but also for the labour of cutting the canes and carrying them to the mill. When, at the end of two years, the mills had been built and the plantations established, another advance was made by the department to the manufacturers. This was capital sufficient to pay for the value of the sugar crop, estimated as it stood, for the wages of the peasants, and generally for the expenses of manufacture. This second advance was at once repaid by the produce of the mill. At first the department required the manufacturer to deliver the whole amount of produce to them at a price one-third in excess of the cost of production. Subsequently he was allowed the option of delivering the whole crop to Government, or of delivering so much of the produce only as would pay for the interest on the crop advance, together with the instalment of the original capital annually due. Working on these terms, large profits were made by the manufacturers, and there soon came to be a demand for such new contracts as the Government had at their disposal.

A PRODUCE MILL.

As for the peasants, they were undoubtedly benefited by the introduction of the system. While the land rent continued to be calculated as before, on a basis of the produce of ricefields, the value of the sugar crop was so much greater than that of the rice, which it partially displaced, that the money received for it amounted on the average to twice the sum paid to Government for land rent on the whole of the village land. Moreover, although the estimated price of the crop was paid to the wedanas, or village chiefs, the wages for cutting and carrying were paid to the peasants individually. The value of the crop, the rate of wages, and the relations between the peasants and the manufacturers generally, were settled by the contrôleurs.

In 1871, when the culture system was in full operation, there were 39,000 *bouws*, or 70,000 acres, under sugar-cane, giving employment to 222,000 native families, and ninety-seven sugar-mills had been started. One-third of the produce was delivered to Government at the rate of eight florins per picul,[17] and the remaining two-thirds were sold by the manufacturers in open market. In the five years 1866-1870 the Government profit on sugar amounted to rather more than 25,000,000 florins.

Subsequently the cultivation of coffee, indigo, cochineal, tobacco, pepper, tea, and cinchona was added to that of sugar. The system pursued was not identical in the case of all produce. Cochineal, indigo, tea, and tobacco were cultivated in a manner similar to that adopted for sugar. But in the case of coffee, cinnamon, and pepper it was not found necessary to have any manufacturers between the contrôleurs and the peasants. Of these coffee, the most important, is grown on lands having an elevation of from 2000 to 4500 feet. Each head of a family is required to plant a certain number of trees in gardens (the maximum was fixed in 1877 at fifty a year), and to keep a nursery of young trees to replenish the plantations. These gardens and nurseries are all inspected by native and European officials. The process of harvesting the berry is similarly supervised, but after that is accomplished the peasants are left to dry, clean, and sort the berries by themselves, and are allowed to deliver the crop at the coffee stores at their own convenience. Finally, private persons contract for periods of two or three years to pack and transport the coffee to the central stores at the ports. Of the coffee produced on Government account, one-fifth only is sold in Java, and the remainder is sent home to Europe and sold there.

The culture system was so successful as a financial expedient, that between the years 1831 and 1875 the colonial revenue yielded surpluses to Holland amounting to 725,000,000 florins. This total seems the more remarkable when we know that from 1838 onwards, the colonial revenue was charged with 200,000,000 florins of the public debt of Holland, being the proportion borne by Belgium before the separation of the two countries, which took place at that date.

In 1876, however, the long series of surpluses ceased, and they have since been replaced by deficits almost as continuous. These deficits are due to three well-ascertained causes: (1) the Achin war, (2) public works, and (3) the fall in the price of sugar and coffee. In order to show that this remarkable change in the financial fortunes of Java is in no way due to the culture system, it is necessary to go somewhat more into detail.

(1) Before the outbreak of the Achin war in 1873, the average expenditure of the Colonial Government for military purposes was 30,000,000 florins annually. During the period 1873-1884 this expenditure rose to an average of 50,000,000 florins, and the total cost of the war during that period amounted to 240,000,000 florins. Since 1884 the expenditure has been reduced by confining the operations of the troops to such as are purely defensive; even then the average annual expenditure has reached 40,000,000 florins.

(2) Since 1875 the construction of railways and of other public works, notably the harbour works at Tanjong Priok, the port of Batavia, has been undertaken by Government. Since the cost has been paid out of current revenue, and not raised by loans, these works have necessitated a further annual expenditure of 8,000,000 florins. The total sum spent in public works between the years 1875-1884, amounting to 75,000,000 florins, is almost exactly equivalent to the deficit incurred during the same period.

(3) In suffering from the competition of France in sugar, and of Brazil in coffee, Java has not been peculiar. The British West Indian colonies are at the present time most disastrously affected by the bounty-fed sugar industry

of France, and Ceylon is only just learning how to compensate itself for the diminution of its coffee export by the introduction of a new industry—tea.

As for the general progress of the island, it is sufficiently indicated by the fact that since the date (1831) of the introduction of the system, the population has increased from six to twenty-three millions, and the revenue from thirty million florins to one hundred and thirty-two.

Although the culture system has yielded such satisfactory results, it has been gradually abandoned since 1871.

The reason for this change of policy is the feeling that the system, though necessary originally to develop the resources of the island, is at variance with the best interests of the natives, and hinders the introduction of private enterprise and capital. Increased commercial prosperity is expected to compensate for the loss of revenue caused by the withdrawal of the Government from the work of production. In the mean time, it has been found necessary to impose various new and direct taxes. The most important of these is a poll tax on the natives, which has taken the place of the personal services formerly rendered by them on the Government plantations. Originally imposed in 1871, it yielded two and a half million florins in 1886. Another compensating source of revenue is the growth of the verponding. As already mentioned, this is a tax of three-fourths per cent, on the capital value of house property and industrial plant. It is assessed every three years, and therefore is an accurate test of the growth of private wealth invested in the colony. In the fifteen years from 1871 to 1886, the amount yielded by this tax showed a growth of seventy-five per cent.

It is not necessary to detail the various steps by which the Dutch have carried out this policy of abandonment. It is sufficient to note the general result.

To-day all industries, with the exception of coffee, opium, and salt, are free. In the production of the two latter, opium and salt, the Colonial Government maintains a complete monopoly; in the case of coffee they compete with the planters. The extent of the shares respectively taken by the Government and private enterprise in the trade of the island is exhibited by the following returns for 1889:—

	IMPORTS.		EXPORTS.	
Government	13,009,445	florins	33,072,175	florins
Private Persons	160,375,326	"	164,590,439	"
Total	173,384,771	"	197,662,614	"

The Government still produces two-thirds of the coffee crop. In 1889 the amount produced respectively by the Government and the planters was 578,000 and 356,000 piculs.

Of the two chief industries of the island, sugar and coffee, the exports in 1890 amounted in value to fifty and fifteen million florins respectively. To these must be added two new industries—tea and cinchona bark. The former is only in its infancy, and is confined to the immediate neighbourhood of Soekaboemi, the head-quarters of the planting interest in Java. Here there are two important estates, Sinagar and Parakan Salak, which are from 12,000 to 15,000 acres in extent. The latter industry is especially hopeful. In 1890 the area of cinchona plantations was 22,500 acres, and 6,000,000 pounds of bark, containing four per cent, of sulphate of quinine, was exported. This amount is equivalent to half the world's supply for the year.

Of the import trade it is not necessary to say more than that the most important item is that of the various cotton goods, coming mainly from this country, which serve the natives with material for clothing suitable for their tropical climate. It is also important to remember that there are a quarter of a million Chinese residents in the island, by whom all the retail, and part of the wholesale, trade is conducted.

Last year the administration of Java was the subject of a severe criticism in the Netherlands Parliament. The complaints were chiefly directed against the conduct of the Achin war, the opium monopoly, and the continued interference of the Government in the coffee industry. The reply of Baron Mackay, the colonial minister at the Hague, was in substance as follows:—

The Achin war, he said, was the result of unavoidable circumstances, and neither the Colonial nor the Home Government could be regarded as responsible for the loss of revenue involved in it. He added, however, that "excellent results were expected from the blockade system" now adopted, and that there were already signs that the Atchinese would before long be brought to terms. With regard to the sale of opium, he assured the States-General that "every possible means were being taken to reduce the sale of the drug, and to remedy its evil effects." He frankly recognized the importance of the question of coffee-culture, but at the same time urged the advisability of maintaining the system for the present. It was not certain, in the first place, that the existing system could be changed with advantage; and, in the second, "no product in the immediate future could be looked for to replace coffee as a source of revenue."

Undoubtedly the resources of Java are at the present time subjected to a heavy strain. On the other hand, it must not be forgotten that (1) the burden of the Achin war may be at any time removed, and (2) all public works are being paid for out of current revenue without recourse to loans. There is, therefore, no reasonable ground for supposing that the present financial difficulties of the Colonial Government are more than temporary. A glance at the balance-sheet of the island for the year 1889 shows to what an extent the difficulties are due to an increasing sense of responsibility towards the natives, and to an intention to eventually open all the industries of this singularly fertile island to private enterprise.

HEADS OF REVENUE AND EXPENDITURE FOR 1889 IN
MILLION FLORINS.

Revenue.		*Expenditure.*	
Taxes	40	Instruction	10
Monopolies	31	Army and navy	40
Sale of produce (of this coffee contributes 37, sugar 2)	49	Public works (of this railways cost 10)	20
Other sources (railways, school fees, etc.)	14	Administration, etc.	60
In round numbers	134		130

When the natives have been educated and the industries of the island freed from unnatural restrictions, financial and commercial prosperity will return to Java.

Footnotes:

[16] 12 florins = £1.

[17] The picul = 135 lbs.

CHAPTER X.
ON A COFFEE PLANTATION.

The Tji Wangi bungalow—Coffee plantations— Cinchona—Native labour—A wayang—Country-bred ponies—Bob and the ducks—Loneliness of a planter's life.

Horace's remark,[18] "Those that cross the sea change temperature, not temperament," is especially true of the Englishman out of England. The room in which I was now seated differed in scarcely anything from the regulation "den" of every Englishman, whether in Scotland or Timbuctoo. From the French windows I could see smooth lawns and bright flower-beds, while beyond appeared the dark green plantations surmounted with grey mountain heights. Photographic groups and etchings shared the task of decorating the walls with riding-gear and Indian knives. The writing-table was strewn with photograph-frames of all sorts and sizes. The black "boy" who brought tea and whisky and Apollinaris, alone gave a hint of "foreign parts." The house itself stood 3500 feet above sea-level; but some of the estate (which covered 800 acres) rose nearly 1000 feet higher still. At this altitude the temperature was never excessively hot: at midday it averaged 70°; certainly it never approached the heat of Batavia; and that night I did what I had not done before in Java—slept with a blanket over me.

The next morning, two handsome Sandalwood ponies were brought round, and H—— took me over the estate. We rode between coffee and cinchona plantations on roads of various widths cut in zigzags or curves up the mountain sides, sometimes with the sun blazing full above us, sometimes shaded by the light foliage of the albizzias, until we reached a rough stone monument which marked the highest point. In the higher ranges we sometimes came upon a piece of bush with the tall rosamala trees still standing; or caught a glimpse of wide plains, bounded in the far-off distance by lofty mountains.

ROSAMALA TREES.

On more than one occasion H—— stopped to talk to the natives. They were engaged in weeding—the heaviest work on the plantation, since, in the hothouse atmosphere of Java, continual labour is required to keep down the rapidly growing plants of all kinds, which would otherwise impoverish the soil and choke the coffee trees. He usually addressed the *mandors*, or native foremen, but once or twice he spoke sharply to an idle or careless worker. His method, he explained, was to treat them with strict justice, but merciless severity: both were necessary to secure their respect, adding that it was useless for a man who was not respected to have anything to do with native labour.

It was during many such rides, supplemented by visits to the factory and long after-dinner talks with many different persons, that I learnt something of the ins and outs of a planter's life.

Although the Dutch Government are gradually abandoning the "culture" or "Government-plantation" system, the change is too recent to permit as yet of the full development of private enterprise in the island. Even now there are Government plantations in every village, in which the natives are compelled to work without wages. Of course, it is easy to undersell the planters by produce raised on these conditions. In addition to the direct Government competition, they complained of export duties on their coffee and cinchona, and of *ad valorem* property taxes upon their plantations and buildings. Altogether, I gathered, the planters considered themselves very badly treated; but they had just formed an association in order to maintain their interests, and to take concerted action against the assistant-residents and the officials generally, who sometimes failed to appreciate the benefit conferred upon the country by the making of roads and other similar improvements.

The average size of the Javan coffee plantations is from 400 to 500 acres. At Tji Wangi there were 500 acres laid down in coffee, and 300 in cinchona. Part of the plantation was new, and H—— had done some clearing since he had taken over the estate. He described the process. The first thing to be done was to clear the forest. The trees were felled; the light timber—underwood and branches—was removed or burnt, but the huge trunks, bare and blackened, were left upon the ground. Indeed, I saw many such trunks, affording a curious contrast to the young plants growing around them. After this, he had formed plantations of albizzias (a slight, tall tree, with a foliage resembling that of the accacia), and planted the young trees, when they were sufficiently grown, at intervals upon the ground he had just cleared. Finally, the coffee trees, which had been grown from seedlings, and had remained in the nurseries for a year, were planted in rows, six or seven feet apart, under the shelter thus provided for them by the albizzias. The coffee trees do not bear until their third year. At the fifth year they reach maturity, and then continue in their prime for as long as ten or fifteen years. Those grown upon the higher, and therefore cooler, ranges will sometimes remain in first-rate condition for even a longer time.

H—— gathered a branch to show me the berry. It was like an acorn with the cup taken off in shape, and of a reddish-brown colour. These berries are harvested ordinarily at the beginning of the dry monsoon, *i.e.* in April or May. As the coolies are paid in proportion to the amount they gather, the whole crop is first of all measured. It is then put into a pulping-machine, and the husk or outer covering removed. The coffee is now said to be in the parchment, *i.e.* the two lobes of the bean are still covered by a parchment-like skin, and in this condition the bean is washed down into the fermenting-tanks, where it remains for thirty-six hours. After a final washing, it is dried in the sun in large wooden trays running on wheels, or else on concrete platforms. Most of the Javan coffee is sent off to Europe while it is still in the husk, in order that it may present a better appearance in the European markets. At Tji Wangi, however, the whole work of preparation was done on the estate.

As is well known, the civilized world is indebted for its increased supply of quinine to Mr. Charles Ledger, the naturalist. In a subsequent chapter I have given Mr. Ledger's interesting account of the manner in which he succeeded, after various adventures, in the course of which occurred the death of his faithful Indian servant, Manuel, in procuring a small quantity of *Cinchona calisaya* seed from Bolivia, part of which was sold to the British and part to the Dutch East India Governments. It is from the nurseries thus formed that the plantations of Java and Ceylon were stocked.

In Java the cinchona is ordinarily grown by grafting slips from a hybrid or *Ledgeriana* of known quality on to the *Succirubra* stem. The succirubra grows fast, but yields only a small percentage of quinine; the hybrid contains from ten to sixteen per cent. of sulphate of quinine. By this device a combination of quick growth and good bearing qualities is obtained, since the hybrid thus formed bears as freely as the graft. The cinchona crop is harvested whenever it is convenient, independently of the seasons, but generally at the same time as the coffee. The quinine is contained in the bark of the tree. The first crop of a plantation consists of branch bark. After the plants have been growing for about six years, a whole row is taken out. In this case the trees are entirely removed not 'barked' at all, and the whole of the bark, even that of the roots, is utilized. It is separated from the wood by beating the stems with sticks or wooden hammers. This is done by women, who sit in circles round large trays, into which they drop the bark as it falls off. It is then left to dry, and afterwards collected and placed in long wooden troughs, where it is stamped fine with heavy wooden stampers. In this condition it is packed into round bales. Finally, both coffee and cinchona are transported by coolies to the nearest railway station.

WOMEN BARKING CINCHONA.

It is in respect of labour that the Javan planters have an advantage over those of Ceylon. At Tji Wangi from 125 to 600 coolies were employed according to the season of the year. They were paid at the rate of 20, 15, and 10 cents (or 4*d.*, 3*d.*, and 2*d.*) respectively for a man, woman, or child per day; the mandors, or foremen, however, received from 30 to 40 cents per day. Yet so simple and cheap are the necessaries of life in Java, that in this district a good master has no difficulty in getting Javanese or Sundanese natives to work for him at this rate of payment, and the plantation cooly, in spite of his low wages, manages to enjoy his two days' holiday every week in the year.

H—— said that the average cost of living per head among his coolies was not more than 10 cents, or 2*d.*, per day. It should be added, however, that the rate of wages varies in the different residencies. In those in which there are large towns, especially in the eastern districts, the native workers, both coolies and artisans, are paid at a considerably higher rate than they are in the Preanger Regencies.

I have already mentioned the wayang as one of the most popular amusements of the natives, and I shall have something more to say about it in connection with the native literature. At Tji Wangi I had an opportunity of witnessing this performance in its simplest form, *i.e.* the wayang *klitik*, in which the puppets are exhibited themselves to the audience instead of being made to project shadows on a transparent screen. Here, as at most plantations, it was customary for the weekly market, held after pay-day, to be followed by a wayang.

When I reached the factory I found that the wages were being paid. The coolies were seated (or rather squatted) on the ground in rows inside the coffee-washing shed, while H—— sat at a table, with his manager and foremen standing round him. After receiving their wages, the crowd of natives flocked through the factory gates to an open space in front of the storehouse. Here the different itinerant vendors had already arranged their goods on stalls or on the ground. There were all manner of cottons and silks, trinkets and hardwares. In addition to these, queer edibles were to be seen— little dishes of pickled vegetables and cured fish, fruits and cakes, even gold-fish. These latter were kept in vessels filled with water, so that the fish could be put back into the ponds again if they were not sold.

A DALANG.

It was a pretty scene, this crowd of bright-coloured humanity. The skin of the Javanese is little darker than that of the Italian, and his clothes are gloriously picturesque. As usual, the hats, jackets, scarfs, and sarongs displayed every shade of colour and variety of pattern. The wayang did not begin until the evening. The chief performer, called the *dalang*, or manager, squatted on the ground before two poles of bamboo placed horizontally at a height of about three feet, into which he stuck the puppets, taking them from a box placed by his side. He chanted a long legendary tale taken from the ancient Javan literature, and dealing with the times before the European occupation of the island. At intervals he broke into a dialogue, when he worked the puppets' arms and legs with wires, so that they seemed to be acting their several parts. Behind the dalang was a *gamelan*, or series of gongs mounted on a wooden frame much like an ordinary couch. These gongs were struck with wooden hammers by other members of the company, and thus served as an orchestra. It was interesting to observe the deep attention with which the audience followed the movements of the puppets, and listened to the recitations and dialogue. H—— said they would sit there listening for hours, far into the night, without getting tired.

Owing to the restrictive trade policy of the Government, the planters, as a class, are much more identified with the native princes than with the Dutch officials. In a subsequent chapter I shall have occasion to speak of the development of horse-racing in Java, and of the support which is given to the movement by the native princes. At Tji Wangi I was shown a recent importation from Sydney—Lonely, who was destined to lower the colours of the Regent of Tjandjoer recently carried to victory by Thistle, also an Australian horse. The stables (like everything else in Java) were built of bamboo. They were kept in first-rate order. The stalls were occupied chiefly by country-bred ponies, the progeny of the native races of the neighbouring islands of Sandalwood and Timor. H—— said modestly that his stud was a very small one, but that if I would visit a Dutch neighbour I should see a stud of fifteen racers, beside brood mares. Race meetings and the various social gatherings connected with them are among the most important resources of the planter's life. H——'s nearest European neighbours were seven miles away, and he said that he could seldom entertain visitors at Tji Wangi, because of the scarcity of game in the neighbourhood. Indeed, the loneliness of the life is its great objection. The case of the Dutch planters is rather different. They are often married, and with their managers, form quite a little society of their own. But an Englishman rarely has the courage to bring a wife so far from home. In most cases it is the near prospect of returning with a fortune which alone makes so isolated an existence bearable.

Under these circumstances, it was not strange that H—— should keep a number of canine pets. Among them Bob, an English bulldog, was his favourite. He was as good-natured as he was ugly, seldom misbehaving, even when tempted beyond doggish endurance by the proximity of dark skins and waving drapery. On one occasion, however, he did give way to anger; but it must be admitted that he had provocation. H—— had some black ducks which he had carefully reared to ornament the little lake in the garden. One afternoon, when Master Bob was taking his siesta in the neighbourhood of the kitchen, with his small white teeth protruding, after the manner of bulldogs, from his black lips, and gleaming in the light, an unfortunate duck came by. Seeing the white oblong-masses in the region of Bob's mouth, she very naturally concluded that they were grains of rice left by the careless quadruped. Acting upon this theory, she hastily essayed to seize the morsel. The impact of her bill upon his nose woke Bob in terrible indignation. A short scuffle and a plaintive quack, and that duck's career was ended. But that was not all. So serious did the bulldog consider this insult to his dignity that, in spite of repeated castigations, he never rested until he had killed the whole of the remaining brood of ducks.[19]

Bob's predecessor in office had been poisoned by a native cook. "But I got her two months," H—— added, "and told my people that I had sent for another bulldog from England, and that if they poisoned *him* I should send for six more."

"But you once told me you had your house broken into. How did that happen?" This was in one of our talks in the smoking-room after dinner.

"It wasn't a very exciting business," he replied. "All I know was that the money was gone the next morning. The night before I was very tired and slept soundly; when I woke up I found my despatch-box gone. I summoned my people and set them to look for it; it was found about a hundred yards away, with the papers in it, but the money gone. About a month afterwards I discovered that one of the natives had been spending more money than he could account for, and, by the help of the native police, I got him convicted and sentenced to transportation for four years. There were three men concerned, but the others escaped through insufficient evidence. One of the stable boys had pulled up the bolts of the front door, and the thieves had quietly walked in, taken the box outside, and broken it open. It was a mere accident—my putting the money into the despatch-box instead of into the safe; but, of course, I took precautions against a repetition of the affair. I had my safe fastened into the ground, and the two safes at the office were built into the wall, as you saw.

"Now, you see, they know there's always a revolver here"—pointing to the desk—"and another by my bedside at night. There are a couple of guns there, but of course they would not be any good, although the bowie-knife hanging by them would. I always have two dogs in the house, one here and one in my bedroom, and there are five or six outside."

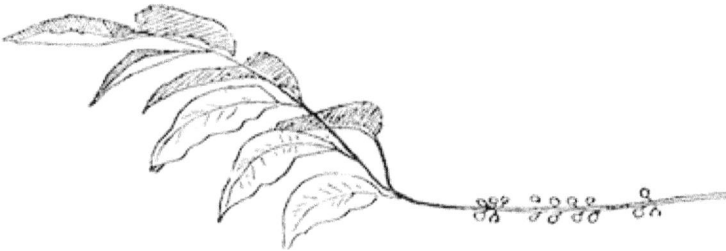

COFFEE BERRIES.

CHAPTER XI.
ANIMAL AND PLANT LIFE.

Mr. Wallace and the Malay Archipelago—Animals— Birds—General characteristics of plants—European flora in mountains—Darwin's explanation—Fruits— History of cinchona introduction—Mr. Ledger's story—Indiarubber.

No less than eight years (1854—1862) were employed by Mr. Wallace, the naturalist, in "the study of man and nature" in the Malay Archipelago. During this period he collected a vast number of specimens of animals and plants, and, some years after his return to England, gave the results of his travels to the world in his "Malay Archipelago." The general conclusions which Mr. Wallace was led to form are of such interest, that I shall endeavour very briefly to lay them before the reader.

In the first place, the evidence supplied by the nature of the distribution of the various plants and animals is such as to point to the belief that the whole Archipelago is composed of fragments of two separate continents. The Malay islands must, therefore, be divided into two groups. Of these groups the first, roughly consisting of Sumatra, Java, Borneo, and the Philippines, once formed part of the continent of Asia; while in the second, the Celebes, Flores, Timor, the Moluccas, and New Guinea, we have fragments of a great Pacific continent, which has been gradually and irregularly broken up. The inhabitants of the former region, to which Mr. Wallace gives the name Indo-Malayan, are Malays; those of the latter, the Austro-Malayan, are Papuans.

Secondly, the intervening seas, which surround the various islands which have now taken the place of these former continental tracts, have been formed by the subsidence of land from which the foundations have been withdrawn by the continued activity of a long volcanic chain which traverses the Archipelago from end to end. And therefore, strange as it may seem at first sight, the fertile island of Java, with its rich plains and abundant vegetation—so unlike the traditional barrenness of a volcanic region—is the work of this subterranean energy.

"The island of Java contains more volcanoes, active and extinct, than any other known district of equal extent. They are about forty-five in number, and many of them exhibit most beautiful examples of the volcanic cone on a large scale, single or double, with entire or truncated summits, and averaging 10,000 feet high."[20]

Thirdly, not only did Sumatra, Java, and Borneo once form part of the continent of Asia, but the subsidence of land which caused their separation from the continent, and from each other, is of very recent date—recent, that is, in the scale of geological eras. This is shown by the fact that the separating seas are so shallow that to-day ships can anchor anywhere in them. We shall, therefore, expect a strong similarity, almost amounting to a complete identity, to exist between the animals and plants of Sumatra, Java, and Borneo and those of Southern India, Burmah, and the Malay Peninsular. Such, according to Mr. Wallace, is the fact.

"The elephant and tapir of Sumatra and Borneo, the rhinoceros of Sumatra and the allied species of Java, the wild cattle of Borneo, and the kind long supposed to be peculiar to Java, are now all known to inhabit some part or other of Southern Asia.... Birds and insects illustrate the same view, for every family and almost every genus of these groups found in any of the islands occurs also in the Asiatic continent, and in a great number of cases the species are exactly identical."

In addition to the rhinoceros and wild cattle mentioned above, the wild animals of Java include the jackal, the tiger, and several species of monkeys. Snakes and alligators are also to be found in the island. There is a good supply of domestic animals with the exception of sheep. This useful animal was so entirely unknown to the natives, that when the Dutch attempted to introduce it into the island it was necessary to find a name for it. It was accordingly called a "Dutch goat;" nor is there at the present time any other term in the Malay language by which the animal can be designated. I have already spoken of the utility of the Javan horses. They are imported in large numbers from the neighbouring island of Sandalwood, and great attention is being paid to the production of country-breds. An attempt is also being made to improve the breed by the importation of English and Australian thoroughbreds. I was also informed that in recent years a number of cattle had been introduced from India. As in most Eastern countries, the ox is used in Java for drawing carts and for other agricultural purposes; but the buffalo is the most valuable of all animals to the natives, by whom it is especially employed in the cultivation of the ricefields. The only dangerous animal is the tiger, and the sport of tiger-hunting still forms one of the recreations of the native princes.

The birds of Java are distinguished for their variety and for the rich plumage with which they are adorned. During a single month passed in Ardjoeno, a mountain situated in the regency of Paseroean, in the east of the island, Mr. Wallace collected ninety-eight species of birds. Among these he mentions the Javan peacock, of which he obtained two specimens more than seven feet long; the jungle fowl (*Gallus furcatus*); the jungle cock (*Gallus bankiva*), called by the natives bekéko; various species of woodpeckers and kingfishers; a hornbill (*Buceros lunatus*) more than four feet long; and a "pretty little lorikeet (*Loriculus pusillus*) scarcely more than as many inches." When he visited the west of the island, he found still more valuable specimens in the Preanger regencies, twenty miles south of Buitenzorg. Among the mountains of this neighbourhood, and at an elevation of 4000 feet, he collected in a fortnight forty species of birds, "almost all of which were peculiar to the Javanese fauna." In these were included the "elegant yellow-and-green trogon (*Harpactes Reinwardti*); the gorgeous little minivet flycatcher (*Pericrocotus miniatus*), which looks like a flame of fire as it flutters among the bushes; and the rare and curious black-and-crimson oriole (*Analcipus sanguinolentus*)." Mr. Wallace also speaks of the rare and beautiful butterflies which he captured here. In particular he secured a specimen of the calliper butterfly, "remarkable for having on each hind wing two curved tails like a pair of callipers."

It is in this neighbourhood that the large Javan wood-pigeons which I saw at Tji Wangi are to be found. As they are excellent eating, they are shot by the planters, though it is often difficult to get within range of them owing to the height of the rosamala trees in which they settle.

There are certain characteristic developments of plant-life which arrest the attention of the traveller in Java.

In the towns he cannot fail to be impressed with the large-leaved and gorgeously coloured shrubs which surround the houses of the European residents; he will notice, too, that the streets and open spaces are planted with waringin and tamarind trees, and when he travels into the interior he will find that the roads which traverse the island are still lined by the same trees. Of these the former is a species of *ficus*; the latter, the tamarind, has been introduced from Madagascar. Towards the end of the year it is covered with orange blossoms, which finally develop into a somewhat acid fruit. In the country the dwellings of the Javan peasants are almost universally surrounded by palms, bananas, and bamboos. While the palms and bananas supply the native with fruit, from the bamboo he has learnt to make numberless useful articles, ranging from a house or a boat to a drinking-vessel or a musical instrument. Cooking-utensils, baskets, hats, and all manner of tools are constructed out of the material provided by this useful tree. While I was staying at a friend's house at Weltevreden I had a singular illustration of the variety of uses to which the bamboo could be put by observing the method of cutting the grass adopted by a native gardener. He was squatting on the ground, and had by his side about half a dozen sections into which he had split some bamboo rods about two feet in length. These he rapidly passed over the grass backwards and forwards with a semicircular sweep, and their sharp edges mowed the grass down as cleanly as the blade of a scythe. In this way he cleared a space around him, and, gradually advancing, eventually trimmed off the whole plot of grass.

The tropical forests, again, are characterized by a remarkable uniformity and sombreness which gives them an aspect quite unlike that of European woods. The vast cylindrical trunks of the great forest trees, rising like pillars from the midst of ferns and lesser growths, support a lofty roof of leaves. Beneath this screen innumerable forms of plant-life develop without let or hindrance, and the whole abundant foliage is bound into an inextricable mass by parasites and creepers. On every side the eye is met by one monotonous tone of verdure, for the supremely favourable conditions for plant-life which obtains tend to produce a total effect, not of variety, but of sameness.

One of the most interesting facts connected with the Javan flora is the appearance of European flowers upon the higher levels of the mountains. The phenomenon is the more remarkable in the face of the consideration that the seeds of such flowers are so heavy, and the distance from their present habitat so great, as to negative the supposition that they have been carried by the wind; nor can their presence be satisfactorily referred to the agency of birds.

At first sight, therefore, the existence of flowers such as the violet, the buttercup, and the honeysuckle in an island south of the equator, and surrounded by vegetation of a totally different order, appeared to be so inexplicable that the hypothesis of a separate and distinct origin was advanced. A more satisfactory explanation has, however, been furnished by Darwin, which is now generally accepted. Very briefly, this is as follows. It is supposed that at the time of the glacial epoch the depression of temperature was so great as to admit of the prevalence in the tropics of forms of plants now peculiar to the temperate regions of the north. As the heat increased, such plants retreated from the tropics, for the most part northwards, but not exclusively. Following the snow-line, they also climbed to the cool heights of the lofty mountains of Central India and of Abyssinia, and even crossed the equator. They now linger upon the summits of the Javan mountains, and furnish by their presence an additional proof of the original union of the western islands of the Archipelago with the continent of Asia.

During his stay at Buitenzorg, Mr. Wallace ascended the mountains Pangerango and Gedé. He describes this expedition as "by far the most interesting incident" of his visit to Java, and gives a full account of the various European plants which he found growing at different altitudes. In particular he mentions the royal cowslip (*Primula imperialis*), "which is said to be found nowhere else in the world but on this solitary mountain summit," and the stem of which he found sometimes growing to a height of over three feet. The list of families of European plants growing upon Pangerango and Gedé given by another scientific traveller, Mr. Motley, includes, among others, such familiar names as the violet, the buttercup, the primula, the lily of the valley, the honeysuckle and the wood-sorrel. I have already mentioned the fact that it is found possible to grow all European plants (but not fruits) in the mountain garden which is established on the slopes of Gedé, and which forms part of the Government gardens.

Of the tropical fruits in general I am inclined to think that their excellences have been very much over-estimated. There is nothing to equal or approach a fine jargonelle pear, a peach, or hothouse grapes. The orange, cocoanut, banana, and mango are so well known as to need no special description. In addition to these, the commonest fruit are the pomelo, the mangosteen, the duku, the rambutan, and the durian. The pomelo is six or seven inches in diameter, with a smooth green exterior, not unlike that of a water-melon; the fruit is pink in colour, and easily breaks up into sections. It tastes like a very dry and rather acid orange, and the peel makes an excellent bitter in sherry. The rambutan resembles a horse-chestnut in size and appearance, except that its shaggy exterior is red instead of green. The duku and mangosteen, on the other hand, are smooth and green, and in other respects resemble a walnut. All three, rambutan, duku, and mangosteen, provide a gelatinous substance with a delicate acid flavour. The durian is as large as a cocoa-nut, and its exterior is armed with spikes; the fruit is soft and pulpy, tasting like a custard in flavour, but it has a horrible smell, and possesses strong laxative qualities. Mr. Wallace devotes several pages to a description of its various qualities, remarking that "to eat durians is a new sensation, worth a voyage to the East to experience." *Credat Judæus non ego.* There is also a species of green orange, with a very thin skin and fine acid flavour, to be obtained in Java.

A general view of the products of the island has already been given in Junghuhn's table in Chapter II., and some of the more important have been subsequently described at length. Any account of the plants of Java would, however, be incomplete without a narrative of the introduction of cinchona into the East Indies.

This plant, from the bark of which quinine is obtained, is a native of Peru, and for a long time the Peruvian Government jealously maintained exclusive possession of it. Forty years ago, the Dutch Colonial Government despatched Haskarl, one of the officials of the Buitenzorg gardens, to Peru for the purpose of procuring cinchona seed. He succeeded in obtaining some seed of a very inferior quality, and the plantations produced from it were practically useless. In 1866, however, both the British and Dutch Indian Governments purchased small quantities of seed from Mr. Charles Ledger. From this seed the very valuable plantations of Java and Ceylon have been propagated. I have already described the method of cultivating *Cinchona Ledgeriana* adopted by the planters, and how advantage is taken of the extreme liability of the cinchona plant to hybridization. The manner in which the seed was secured forms an interesting episode in the history of scientific botany. The story is told by Mr. Ledger in a letter to his brother published in the *Field* of Feb. 5, 1881, in which it will be seen that these seeds were obtained at the cost of the life of Manuel, the naturalist's faithful Indian servant.

"While engaged in my alpaca enterprise of 1856, a Bolivian Indian, Manuel Tucra Mamami, formerly and afterwards a cinchona bark-cutter, was accompanying me with two of his sons. He accompanied me in almost all my frequent journeys into the interior, and was very useful in examining the large quantities of cinchona bark and alpaca wool I was constantly purchasing. He and his sons were very much attached to me, and I placed every confidence in them. Sitting round our camp-fire one evening, as was our custom after dinner, conversing on all sorts of topics, I mentioned what I had read as to Mr. Clement R. Markham's mission in search of cinchona seeds. Now, Manuel had been with me in three of my journeys into the cinchona districts of the Yungas of Bolivia, where I had to go looking after laggard contractors for delivery of bark. It was while conversing on the subject of Mr. Markham's journey, and wondering which route he would take, etc., that Manuel greatly surprised me by saying, 'The gentleman will not leave the Yungas in good health if he really obtains the *rogo* plants and seeds.' Manuel was always very taciturn and reserved. I said nothing at the time, there being some thirty more of my Indians sitting round the large fire. The next day he reluctantly told me how every stranger on entering the Yungas was closely watched unobserved by himself; how several seed-collectors had their seed changed; how their germinating power was destroyed by their own guides, servants, etc. He also showed me how all the Indians most implicitly believe, if, by plants or seeds from the Yungas, the cinchonas are successfully propagated in other countries, all their own trees will perish. Such, I assure you, is their superstition. Although there are no laws prohibiting the cinchona seed or plants being taken out of the country, I have seen private instructions from the prefect in La Paz ordering strictest vigilance to prevent any person taking seed or plants out of the country. More than half a dozen times I have had my luggage, bedding, etc., searched when coming out of the valley of the Yungas.

"You are aware how I am looked upon as a doctor by the Indians. Well, one day I said, 'Manuel, I may some day require some seed and flowers of the famous white flower, *Rogo cascarrilla*, as a remedy; and I shall rely upon you not deceiving me in the way you have told me.' He merely said, 'Patron, if you ever require such seed and flowers, I will not deceive you. And I thought no more about it.

"Manuel was never aware of my requiring seed and leaves for propagating purposes; he was always told they were wanted to make a special remedy for a special illness. For many years, since 1844, I had felt deeply interested in seeing Europe, and my own dear country in particular, free from being dependent on Peru or Bolivia for its supply of life-giving quinine. Remembering and relying on Manuel's promise to me in 1856, I resolved to do all in my power to obtain the very best cinchona seed produced in Bolivia.

"His son Santiago went to Australia with me in 1858. In 1861, the day before sending back to South America Santiago and the other Indians who had accompanied me there as shepherds of the alpacas, I bought 200 Spanish dollars, and said to him, 'You will give these to your father. Tell him I count on his keeping his promise to get me forty to fifty pounds of rogo cinchona (white flower) seed. He must get it from trees we had sat under together when trying to reach the Mamore river in 1851: to meet me at Tacna (Peru) by May, 1863. If not bringing pure, ripe rogo seed, flowers, and leaves, never to look for me again.'

"I arrived back in Tacna on the 5th of January, 1865. I at once sent a message to Manuel, informing him of my arrival. At the end of May he arrived with his precious seed. It is only now, some twenty-four years after poor Manuel promised not to deceive me, manifest how faithfully and loyally he kept his promise. I say *poor* Manuel, because, as you know, he lost his life while trying to get another supply of the same class of seed for me in 1872-3. You are aware, too, how later on I lost another old Indian friend, poor Poli, when bringing seed and flowers in 1877.

"I feel thoroughly convinced in my own mind that such astonishingly rich quinine-yielding trees as those in Java are not known to exist (in any quantity) in Bolivia. These wonderful trees are only to be found in the Caupolican district in Eastern Yungas. The white flower is specially belonging to the cinchona 'rogo' of Apolo.

"You will call to mind, no doubt, the very great difficulties you had to get this wonderful 'seed' looked at, even; how a part was purchased by Mr. Money for account of our East Indian Government for £50 under condition of 10,000 germinating. Though 60,000 plants were successfully raised from it by the late Mr. McIver, I only received the £50.

"The seed taken by the Netherlands Government cost it barely £50.

"Such, then, is the story attaching to the now famous *Cinchona Ledgeriana*, the source of untold wealth to Java, Ceylon, and, I hope, to India and elsewhere. I am proud to see my dream of close on forty years ago is realized; Europe is no longer dependent on Peru or Bolivia for its supply of life-giving quinine."

Before closing this chapter I may mention that there is a considerable plantation of gutta-percha trees in the horticultural garden at Buitenzorg. The best producer of gutta-percha, *Pelaguium (isonandra) Gutta*, grows nowhere on the island naturally, but seeds were obtained from two specimens of this plant which had been placed in the botanical garden, and the plantation was established some years ago at the suggestion of Dr. Treub. In view of the recent development of electrical engineering and the increased demand for indiarubber generally which has arisen in the last few years, the fact that an unlimited supply of this valuable plant can be obtained in Java is one of some importance to the commercial world.

Footnotes:

[20] "Malay Archipelago."

CHAPTER XII.
SOCIAL LIFE.

Dutch society in the East—Batavian etiquette— English residents—
Clubs—Harmonie—Concordia— Lawn-tennis—Planters—Horse-racing.

Boston is not the only place in the world which has decided upon insufficient
evidence that it is the centre of the universe. We all of us have a weakness
for the special form of civilization with which we are most familiar, and to
discover excellences of character and manners essentially identical with those
we have been taught to associate with a cherished society in our own country,
in places where we least expect them, is part of the discipline of travel. In the
Dutch over-sea settlements society is more exclusive and regulated by a more
rigid code of etiquette than it is in Holland. Nor will it seem strange, when
the special conditions of Javan life are remembered, that the persons
composing this society should be indolent, luxurious, and imperious. On the
other hand, an abundance of leisure, and a consciousness of racial superiority
acquired by habits of command exercised for several generations, endow it
with some of the finer qualities associated with ancient society based upon
the institution of slavery.

Nor must we forget that the Dutch are not mere "birds of passage" in Java,
as is the case with the English in India. On the contrary, the majority of the
Dutch residents are persons whose families have been settled in the island
for many generations, and who look upon Java as their home. One has only
to look round in the streets of Weltevreden to realize the fact that Batavia is
a colony, not merely a possession. From seven to eight in the morning,
troops of boys and girls are to be seen going to school. The little girls are
dressed in light materials; they do not wear either hats or bonnets, and rarely
carry sunshades. The boys wear brown holland trousers and jackets, and the
military cap of a continental school. Although children are sent to Holland
for social reasons, the climate of Java does not require that painful separation
of parents and children which is one of the disagreeable accidents of Indian
life. On the contrary, the Dutch race appears to have developed favourably
in Java, and the colonial-born women are famous for the beauty of their
complexions and for the fineness of their physique. Another test of the social
condition of a community is its shops. In Batavia there are excellent shops.
Not merely can the newest books, and the cleverest etchings, and all the
numberless refinements of Bond Street be obtained, but the manners of the
tradespeople indicate that they are accustomed to deal with persons who
require to be served promptly, and with the best.

In addition to the native and Chinese population, there are seven thousand
Europeans resident in Batavia. As most of these latter are persons whose

various employments allow them a good deal of "leisure," there is a corresponding amount of social activity. This is regulated by the rules of old-fashioned continental society, with such innovations as have been rendered necessary or merely suggested by the special conditions of the place and climate. As the official class is the basis upon which Batavian society rests, it is not surprising that ceremony should play an important part in its system. Among European communities in warm countries, a considerable licence is generally allowed in the matter of dress; but in Batavia, etiquette requires a man to wear a frock coat and white gloves for paying a call. Moreover, before a call which is intended to initiate an acquaintance can be made, notice of the caller's intention, and of the day proposed, must first be sent. These formal calls are made from seven to eight in the evening, and it is not considered polite to leave before the hour has expired. During this period iced water is handed round in elegant glasses, furnished with silver trays and tortoiseshell covers. Again, after introduction to an unmarried lady at a dance, a man is required to properly legitimize the acquaintance. In order to do this, he must be presented to the parents of the lady, if this has not already been done, and he is expected also to make the acquaintance of such of her relatives as are resident in the neighbourhood.

At the date of my visit (1890), the English community in Batavia consisted of fifty or sixty men and five ladies. Up to the last ten years there has been an English chaplain at Batavia; but there is some difficulty in raising the necessary stipend, and so the interesting little church is at present deserted. It is only quite recently that the English residents have received any sort of recognition in Batavian society. Now, however, they have succeeded in establishing two institutions—a paper-chase (on horseback) and a lawn-tennis club, which are likely to modify the rigour of its etiquette.

The Dutch are famous for their clubs. These institutions flourish in Java, and in Batavia they contribute materially to the social life of the place. Among many others, the Societeit Harmonie and the Concordia are the most considerable. At both of them frequent concerts and dances are held. In connection with this latter amusement, it was interesting to find that all the dancing at Batavia was done on marble. I was told that it was not considered unpleasant, and that the only wooden floor in the island was in the Governor-General's palace at Buitenzorg. The Harmonie is a large square building, surrounded on two sides with porticos and verandahs, standing at the corner of Ryswyk. The main entrance leads into an extensive hall with white walls and a lofty roof supported by ranges of pillars. On the marble floor are arranged a number of small tables for light refreshments. To the right and left of this hall is the billiard-room and the reading-room. The former contains some twenty or thirty French and English tables; and the latter is well supplied with European papers and magazines. The two rooms are separated from the hall by light wooden screens, which allow the air to circulate freely from one to another, and in this way the whole building is kept pleasantly cool. The Harmonie was founded in 1815 during the British occupation. In 1889, shortly before my visit, a dinner was held commemorating the foundation of the club, and on each menu card an account of the event was printed, taken from the British Government *Gazette* published at the time. Compared with the Concordia, it is a civilian club; for, although this latter does not by any means restrict its membership to officers in the forces, the management is entirely in the hands of the military, who make the neighbourhood of the Waterloo Plain, where the club stands, a sort of military quarter. The Concordia gives an open-air concert every Saturday evening and every alternate Wednesday afternoon.

I went to one of the Saturday evening concerts, and enjoyed it very much. The air was warm and calm, and it was very pleasant to sit under the wide-spreading waringin trees and gaze up at the twinkling brightness of the stars through the screen of leaves. There was quite a crowd of members and their friends promenading or sitting in easy groups round the little iron tables. The kiosks were brilliantly lighted, but through the branches of the waringin trees the soft radiance of the moon could be seen shining upon the dull blue vault of the sky. The performance was given by the staff band, which never leaves Batavia, and is said to be the best in the East Indies. I give the programme:—

I.

1.	FUR'S VATERLAND MARSCH	*C. Millöcker.*
2.	WIENER FRAUEN WALZER	*J. Strauss.*
3.	OUVERTURE JELVA	*F. Reisiger.*
4.	GRUSS AUS DER FERNE INTERMEZZO	*J. Verhulst.*
5.	MARSCH UND CHOR A. D. OPER. DIE ZAUBERFLÖTE	*W. A. Mozart.*
6.	FANTAISIE LA REINE DE SABA	*Ch. Gounod.*

II.

7.	Ouverture Die Frau Meisterin	*Fr. v. Suppé.*
8.	Die Muhle im Schwarzwald	*R. Eilenberg.*
9.	Finale a. d. Oper. Ariele die Tochter der Luft	*E. Bach.*

On Sunday afternoon a military band plays in the centre of the Waterloo Plain, and all Batavia turns out in carriages or on horseback to listen—all Batavia, that is, with the exception of the very select few who keep to themselves almost entirely, or, if they attend a Concordia concert, never leave their carriages. This select few includes the highest officials and their families, personages such as the general and admiral, and the members of the East India Council. There is an interesting fact in connection with the admiral that recalls the time when the supremacy of the sea was the pride of the Dutch nation. The Governor-General, the general of the forces, and the admiral of the fleet all enjoy the title of "Excellency," while they reside in Java; but, whereas the two former cease to be entitled to it when their term of command is over, the admiral is "his Excellency" to the end of his days.

As I mentioned before, the strictness of Batavian etiquette is likely to be modified by the introduction of a pastime so essentially English as lawn-tennis. The courts of the Bataviasche Lawn-tennis Club are in the Zoological Gardens, south of the King's Plain. The club holds numerous tournaments in the course of the year, and competitions are established for both a ladies' and gentlemen's championship. The great majority of the men who play are English, but the ladies are, from the small number of English women in Batavia, almost exclusively Dutch. The holder of the championship of Batavia, and the secretary of the club, in 1890, was an Englishman, Mr. R. L. Burt. In addition to this club, the old Batavia cricket club, which has an excellent ground on the King's Plain, has been practically converted into a men's lawn-tennis club. I was told that as many as six double courts were to be seen in full play on ladies' days at this club. So that it would appear that the Dutch ladies, at all events, have taken very kindly to lawn-tennis.

The style of living in Batavia is very similar to that of European society in India. The cheapness of labour and consequent number of servants give a certain air of luxury to even moderate establishments. The Malay cooks are particularly skilful in the matter of curreys, and in a good house a "rice-table" is a thing to be remembered. The neatness and quickness of the natives generally make them very suitable for the duties of domestic and body servants. A Batavian dinner is served at a late hour in a lofty and spacious apartment, which is one of a series of chambers through which the air freely circulates from the front to the back of the house. From this room the outside world is excluded only by partially drawn blinds, and through the open windows the perfumes of flowers or the sounds of music are borne in upon the guests. After dinner the party return to the portico in the front, which is almost as completely furnished as an inside room, and the rest of the evening is spent practically in the open air.

Beside the officials who are scattered over Java and the Dutch possessions in the East, the planters form an important element in the social life of the island. They are by no means exclusively Dutch, but the class includes a considerable number of Englishmen. Such men are usually drawn from the higher classes in Holland or in England, and are fairly wealthy and refined. Like the sheep farmers of Australia, they are exceedingly hospitable, and their bungalows are often convenient and even luxurious. Often, too, these latter are set in the midst of mountain scenery, and surrounded by charming gardens.

The planters are the representatives of the principle of free commerce, and the natural opponents of the official class. Everywhere among them complaints are heard of the prejudice displayed against private enterprise, and of unnecessary obstacles placed in their way by the contrôleurs and assistant-residents. As I have already mentioned, a planters' union has lately been established for the purpose of protecting the planting interests. It meets at Soekaboemi, and it is hoped that, by means of concerted action, such grievances will be brought more effectively before the Government. After all, the planters are the real producers of the island, and their importance increases every year in proportion as the area of Government plantations is reduced. In many respects the planters are allied with the native princes. To a large extent the two classes lead the same life and share the same pursuits. They are both brought into close connection with the natives, and they both find their chief recreation in various forms of sport.

Horse-racing in particular has of late years developed very considerably. The principal meetings are held at Buitenzorg and at Bandong, the former in June and September, the latter in July. At Bandong the native princes turn out in force, and the native population hold a carnival in the town. One of the greatest patrons of the turf is the Regent of Tjandjoer. At the time of my visit he was the owner of the premier horse in the island—Thistle, whose sire was Teviot of West Australia. The planters round Soekaboemi are also among the principal supporters of horse-racing in Java.

In Java, as elsewhere, they had a grievance. It was said that the owners of big studs of country-breds dominated the arrangements for events, and that the programmes were made up in favour of such native-bred horses to the exclusion of imported stock. Such a policy was regarded as unfavourable to the best interests of horse-racing in Java, since, instead of encouraging the importation of thoroughbreds from Australia and Europe, it tends to perpetuate the native race. The country-bred horse is undoubtedly a handsome-looking animal, but he exhibits a tendency to become weedy and razor-chested, and fails to carry a heavy weight from deficiency of bone. It is also found that the progeny of imported stock decline in quality both in size and stamina. This is the joint effect of climate and inferior food. Horses are trained merely on fresh grass and paddy (*i.e.* the ear and part of the stalk of the rice plant). Bandaging, I was told, was almost unknown; at the same time the animals were generally sound in feet and legs.

The average height of the country-bred horse is 14.3 to 15 hands; and good time over a mile is between 1 min. 52 sec. and 1 min. 55 sec., carrying at the rate of 75 lbs. (Dutch) for 4 feet, and one pound for every quarter of an inch in advance. In other words, a fifteen-hand horse carries about nine stone. There is no system of handicapping, but horses carry weight for inches; so that a horse may defeat a rival any number of times without effecting a change in the weights, and a known winner carries less weight than his defeated rival if the latter is an inch or two above him.

There are no recognized steeplechases, but generally one or two events at each meeting are reserved for gentlemen riders, and private matches are sometimes arranged. In 1888 the commandant at Buitenzorg offered a prize for a cross-country race for the purpose of encouraging riding among the officers. The event, however, was won by an English planter.

The Buitenzorg meetings are attended by all the best people in the island, and on the first day the Governor-General appears in state. The racing is fixed for the morning, and lasts from nine to twelve. It is a rather curious fact that in Java the starter has discarded the universal red flag, and waves a Dutch tricolour instead.

CHAPTER XIII.
THE HINDU JAVANESE LITERATURE.

The Hindu Javanese literature concerned with the past—Javanese alphabet—Extent of Javanese works— Kavi dialect—Krama and Ngoko— The Mahabharata and the Ramayana in Kavi—Native Kavi works—The Arjuna Vivaya—The Bharata Yuddha—Episode of Salya and Satiavati— Ethical poems—The Paniti Sastra— Localization of Hindu mythology in Java.

The literature of a country reflects its life, but under certain conditions. The literature of Java is mainly, but not entirely, concerned with the distant past, when the quiet tide of Eastern life had received as yet no disturbing impulse from the stream of Mohammedan and European conquest. This Hindu Javanese literature tells us of a people far advanced in the essentials of civilization, and reveals the existence of a social system which, though undoubtedly primitive, was at the same time complete and homogeneous. From the date of the Mohammedan conquest onwards, that is to say, for the last four centuries, the national life has been directed by alien forces. During this period but little or nothing has been added to the literature of the country, since the fresh ideas which have been introduced have come from Mohammedan conquerors, who were themselves provided with a sufficient medium of expression, and one which they sought, as a matter of policy, to impress upon the subject races of the island. Beyond enlightening us upon the social system prevalent many hundred years ago, it would seem that a knowledge of their literature could contribute but slightly towards a comprehension of the Javanese. This opinion, however, is modified by the fact that the Kavi literature has been popularized by translation into modern Javanese, and that the mass of the population are still acquainted with its main features by means of these versions accompanied by the representations of the theatre and the wayang. The ideals of conduct conveyed in these epics, romances, legends, and ethical treatises will, therefore, be those with which the Javanese are still familiar, and presumably such as still enlist their sympathies. Besides this general insight into native methods of thought, there are also certain features of their life and of their present relationship to their European conquerors upon which interesting lights are thrown by an acquaintance with the traditions and beliefs enshrined in the ancient literature.

The Javan alphabet, according to the native idea, consists of only twenty consonants. But as a matter of fact, each of these consonants is credited with an inherent vowel sound of *a* (often written *o*) as in *water*; and there are five vowel signs which are attached to the consonants, and so vary the inherent *a*. There are also twenty auxiliary consonant forms, corresponding to the original twenty consonants, which are used in all combinations of consonants. Even this does not exhaust the list, for there still remain a number of double letters, while modifications of the letters of the alphabet are employed for numbers. Speaking of this alphabet as a whole, Crawfurd says[21] that it reaches perfection, since "it expresses every sound in the language, and every sound invariably with the same character, which never expresses but one." He concludes, "In splendour or elegance the alphabet of the Arabs and Persians is probably superior to that of the Javanese; but the latter, it may be safely asserted, surpasses in beauty and neatness all other written characters." Some idea of the extent of the Javanese literature may be gained from the fact that M. Vreede's recently issued account of the Javanese manuscripts in the Leiden University Library[22] gives the names of some five hundred manuscripts, containing no less than one hundred and fifty separate works. And—to come nearer home—the collection of the Royal Asiatic Society contains as many as forty-four Javanese manuscripts, for which the society is mainly indebted to the generosity of Lady Raffles. No little interest and learning have been displayed by continental scholars in the study of these works; but, unfortunately, their valuable treatises, written in German, French, and Dutch, are not easily accessible to English readers. In order to find an account of the Javanese literature in English, we have to go back more than half a century to the works of Raffles and Crawfurd. Fortunately, the former has enriched his "History" with unusually full and interesting extracts from Javanese works. But since Raffles was in Java immense advances have been made, not only in our general knowledge of oriental languages, but especially in the interpretation of literature by means of antiquarian remains. It is not that his account is rendered worthless by these recent researches. On the contrary, in this latest work, Vreede's "Catalogue," we find frequent quotations from Raffles' appendices. At the same time, when we see how much he achieved with his inadequate materials, it is difficult to suppress a feeling of regret that the fuller information, which is available to-day, was not at the disposal of the author of a "History of Java." As I have embodied in the text some extracts from Raffles' translations, it may be well to say a word as to the value of these versions. What Vreede says of a particular passage is true of these renderings in general: "They are not literal translations, but the spirit of the work is well rendered."

In the present chapter we are concerned only with those Hindu Javanese works which are properly entitled to be classed as "literature." They are written in the Kavi or literary language. The term "Kavi" means the language of poetry, and this dialect is composed, to a great extent, of words of Sanscrit origin. Although the knowledge of Kavi was gradually lost after the Hindu supremacy was overthrown by the Mohammedans, modern Javanese contains but few Arabic words, especially differing in this respect from

Malay. Two forms of modern Javanese are employed in everyday speech. First, the language of ceremony, called Krama; and, secondly, the common speech, or Ngoko (meaning literally the thou-ing speech). The Krama contains a considerable number of words derived from Sanscrit and introduced through the Kavi, and an admixture of Malay. It is used by the peasants and artisans in addressing the native princes. The Ngoko is spoken by the common people among themselves, and by the native princes in communication with their inferiors. The existence of this double language explains the fact (of which I have already spoken) that the Dutch have established Malay, and not Javanese or Sundanese, as the medium of communication between Europeans and natives.

The modified Hinduism which existed at the epoch of the Mohammedan conquest (1400-1500, A.D.) retreated very gradually in an easterly direction before the new religion. At the end of the eighteenth century there were still Hindus in Java, and to-day the ancient religion lingers in Bali, a small island off the south-eastern coast. In Bali, therefore, it is natural that we should find the fullest remains of such parts of the Kavi literature as are most closely identified with that of Continental India. Only fragments of the two great Indian epics, the Mahabharata, or "Great War of the Sons of King Bharata," and the Ramayana, or "Adventures of Rama," are found in Java; but in Bali Kavi versions of both appear. Neither of these versions, however; bears the Indian title of the original work. The Mahabharata, which, with its 220,000 lines, is the longest epic in the world, and which Sir Monier Williams calls "a vast cyclopædia of Hindu mythology," is known as "the Parvas." Of the eighteen parvans, or divisions, of the original, eight only are in existence in the Kavi version. Of these the first, *Adiparva*, is the best preserved, says Dr. Van der Tuuk; "but this also," he adds, "abounds in blunders, and especially the proper names have been so altered from their Indian originals as to be hardly recognizable."[23] As the name "War of the Bharatas" is applicable, strictly speaking, to only one-fifth part of the whole poem, it is probable that the great epic was not yet known under this title at the time when it was transported from India to Java.

The Ramayana appears in a slightly changed form in the Kavi version. The original Indian epic is divided into seven *Kandas*, or volumes, which are again subdivided into chapters. The Kavi version, entitled "the Kandas," contains the narrative of the first six Kandas. The seventh, the *Uttara-Kanda*, or supplementary volume, which gives an account of the descendants of Rama after his death, appears in the Kavi as an entirely separate work. It would appear, therefore, that neither of the two Indian epics had reached their final form when they were carried by Hindu colonists to Java. That part of the Mahabharata which afterwards gave the poem its distinctive title had not yet been written, or at least added to the central myth; and the Ramayana then contained only the history of Rama. Both poems appear, however, to have acquired a reputation for unusual sanctity. In Java and Bali both "the Kandas" and "the Parvas" are used as synonymous terms, and mean "the Sacred Books."

The difference between the Kavi and Indian versions of these epics seems to afford additional evidence—if any such were needed—that neither the Mahabharata nor the Ramayana is the work of a single mind, but that both are a collection or compilation of myths.

It is noticeable also that, in spite of the love of dramatic representation manifested so universally among the Javanese, the Indian dramas were not transplanted to Java. Dr. Friederich[24] offers an explanation of this. "Most of the Indian dramas," he says, "are of late times, and perhaps, at the time the Brahmans came to Java, were exclusively found at the courts of the princes."

We come now to the consideration of what may be called, by contradistinction to the direct versions of the Indian epics, the native Kavi works. The character of these poems—for all the Kavi literature is alike written in metre—is in the main mythological and romantic; but there are also to be found among them certain ethical and religious works. Although the subjects, the heroes, and even the metre in many cases, are still Indian, these subjects and heroes have been so completely identified with the local life that the poems are essentially Javanese.

Of the native Kavi works the "Arjuna Vivaya," which gives an account of the ascent of Arjuna to Indra, and of his love for the nymph Urvasi, deserves to stand first from the purity of the dialect in which it is composed. The Indian hero Arjuna, the son of Pandu, who is called by Sir Monier Williams, "the real hero of the Mahabharata," was adopted by the Javanese, and his name was given to one of their mountains. The metre of the poem is Indian in form, and not Javanese, and the date of its composition is fixed by Professor Kern in his "Kawistudien" as the first half of the eleventh century of our era. The fact that it contains but slight traces of Buddhistic thought is important as giving some hint of the date at which Buddhism was introduced in the island. In this respect it differs from the "Arjuna Vijaya," a later poem celebrating the triumph of the same hero over Ravan, the demon king of Ceylon.

The "Bharata Yuddha," or war of the Bharatas, is so closely connected with the sacred Parvas, that it is generally placed by the Javanese at the head of the native Kavi works. It is esteemed the greatest work in the Javanese literature, but it yields in point of antiquity to the "Arjuna Vivaya." Its language also is less pure, and contains a certain admixture of ordinary high Javanese or Krama. A definite date (1195, A.D.) is assigned to it, and the name of its author is said to be Hempu, or M'pu, S'dah. The subject of the poem is identical with that of four of the parvans of the Mahabharata, but the scene is changed from India to Java. It contains an account of the struggle between the Pandavas, or five sons of Pandu, and the Kauravas, or hundred sons of Dhritavashtra, in which the latter are ultimately defeated in their attempt to obtain the kingdom of Ngastina. The scene is laid in the plains around the city Ngastina, or in the city itself. The poem opens with the following lines:—[25]

"In war 'tis the prayer of the brave to annihilate the foe;To see the braids of fallen chiefs scattered like flowers before the wind;To rend their garments, and burn alike their altars and their palaces;Boldly to strike off their heads while seated in their chariots, and thus to obtain renown."

The episode of King Salya, one of the Kaurava princes, and Satiavati, his queen, is singularly romantic, and reveals a high ideal of wifely devotion. The poem relates how Salya steals away from his wife, and sacrifices himself on the field of battle. Then Satiavati wanders over this same field of battle by night in quest of his corpse. A flash of lightning is sent to direct her steps, and when she has found the body of her husband, she addresses the corpse in a speech in which she declares her intention of following his spirit.

"But earth has lost its fleeting charms for meAnd, happy spirit, I will follow thee."

She continues—

"Though widadaris[26] should obey thy call
Reserve for me a place above them all,"

and finally stabs herself.

To her faithful maid Sagandika she says—

"Tell them to think of Satiavati's fate,
And oft the story of her love relate."

But Sagandika also kills herself.

"Then did their happy spirits wing their way
To the fair regions of eternal day."

I conclude the episode by a quotation from the prose rendering given by Raffles, which keeps more exactly to the original, and gives a characteristically Eastern picture of heaven.

"The astonished spirit of Prince Salya quickly said—
"'Uneasy and impatient have I waited for thee among the clouds, with many widadaris, panditas, and diwas.'
"Having taken the princess in his arms, he returns with her by the road which leads to heaven.
"There arrived, they find it extremely beautiful.
"Of silk were the houses, and brilliant were the precious stones.
"Amusing herself, the princess was delighted with the abundance of food which was there.

"Great being the bounty of the Almighty to mankind. And there was no difference susceptible in the ages of those that were there."

I have already mentioned that among the Kavi poems are contained various ethical works. Of these the "Paniti Sastra," or Manual of Wisdom, will serve as an example. Raffles, in his account of this work, says that it contains one hundred and twenty-three stanzas, and that it is said to be contemporary with the Bharata Yuddha. Vreede, in his "Catalogue," says in a note,[27] "Winter mentions the 'Niti Sastra Kawi,' and as its author Prabu Vidayaka, in the time of Aji Saka." As Saka was the commencement of all things in Java, to refer the work to the time of Aji Saka, is practically to say that it is of unknown antiquity. It belongs to the second class of *Tuturs*, or sacred writings, *i.e.* those which were not kept secret by the priests, but which might be read by other castes beside the Brahmans; and there are several versions and translations of it in modern Javanese. The following lines are taken from the Kavi text of this work:—

"As the suraya flower floats in the water, so does the heart exist in a pure body; but let it not be forgotten that the root of the flower holds to the ground, and that the heart of man depends upon his conduct in life.
"As the moon and the stars shed their light by night, and the sun giveth light by day, so should the sayings of a wise man enlighten all around him.
"Deprive not another of the credit which is due to him, nor lower him in the opinion of the world; for the sun, when he approaches near the moon, in depriving her of her light, adds nothing to his own lustre."

There is a modern Javanese version of the "Niti Sastra," of which the following passages are specimens:—

"A man who is ignorant of the sacred writings, is as one who has lost his speech; for when these become the conversation of other men, he will be under the necessity of remaining silent.

"No man can be called good or bad until his actions prove him so.

"It is well known that a man cannot take the goods of this world with him to the grave, and that man, after this life, is punished with heaven or hell, according to the merits of his actions in this life: a man's duty, therefore, requires him to remember that he must die; and if he has been merciful and liberal in this life to the poor, he will be rewarded hereafter."

One and the same principle governs the composition of the mythological and romantic literature of the Hindu epoch, and that of those somewhat similar works in modern Javanese composed after the Mohammedan conquest. The authors of both alike set one main object before them—to exalt the reigning princes by identifying them with the heroes or princes of an anterior epoch; only in the case of the Kavi poems, this anterior epoch is fixed in the cloud-land of Hindu mythology, while after the Mohammedan conquest it becomes merely the preceding era of the Hindu supremacy in Java, which is used as a ladder by which the Hindu cloud-land may be reached. But the nature of the *babads*, or chronicles, the medium by which this object was subsequently effected, and the interesting question of their historical value, are subjects which I must reserve for the succeeding chapter.

Footnotes:

[21] "Indian Archipelago."

[22] "Catalogus van de Javaansche en Madoereesche Handschriften der Leidsche Universiteits-Bibliotheek door A. C. Vreede. Leiden: 1892."

[23] In the *Journal of the Royal Asiatic Society*, xiii. N.S. 1881.

[24] In the *Journal of R. A. S.* vii. N.S.

[25] I am indebted for this and the subsequent versions in the text to Raffles' "History of Java."

[26] Angels.

[27] Page 262.

CHAPTER XIV
WORKS OF THE MOHAMMEDAN PERIOD.

Uncertainty about the history of the Hindu kingdoms given by the chronicles—Character of the *babad*, or chronicle—Its historical value— Brumund's treatment of the babads—Account of the babad "Mangku Nagara"— Prose works—The Niti Praja—The Surya Ngalam— Romances—The Johar Manikam—Dramatic works—The Panjis—Wayang plays—Arabic works and influence—The theatre—The wayang.

The works of the Mohammedan Javanese period include, in addition to translations and versions of all kinds both from the Kavi literature and the Arabic, romances, dramatic works, and plays, intended both for the theatre and the wayang, ethical and legal compilations, and, lastly, the *babads*, or chronicles. It will be convenient to consider these latter first; but before doing so it is necessary to revert for a moment to the historical account which I gave in my opening chapter. It will be remembered that in that account the two Hindu kingdoms of Pajajaran and Majapahit, respectively founded in the west and east of the island, were mentioned as being especially celebrated in the native chronicles. These chronicles, it is true, give us the names and dates of various earlier kingdoms, and a variety of information about their respective dynasties; but for all practical purposes the history of the Hindu period, as at present revealed, may be summed up in a sentence of Crawfurd. From the latter part of the twelfth century to the overthrow of Majapahit (1478), "a number of independent states existed in Java, and the religion of the people was a modified Hinduism." Antiquarian research further tells us that this series of Hindu states commenced in the centre of the island, and that it was closed by the western kingdom of Pajajaran, which existed as early as the first half of the eleventh century, and the eastern kingdom of Majapahit, which was itself succeeded by the first Mohammedan empire of Demak. Remains of the capital cities of both these Hindu kingdoms are in existence. Those of Pajajaran, which are to be found forty miles from Batavia, are exceedingly meagre, and appear to be the work of a primitive epoch. Those of Majapahit, close by Soerabaia, are numerous and magnificent.

But the chronicles which make these kingdoms the subject of their narratives were not composed until the Mohammedan period was well advanced; or, at least, if they had a previous existence, they were then remodelled under the direction of the susunans, or emperors. They have, therefore, to be regarded with considerable suspicion. In the case of the chronicles which relate contemporary events, we are on surer ground. But such is the nature of the Javanese, and such the literary character of the babad, that even here we are by no means certain to meet with actual facts.

The babad is a poem composed in a common Javanese measure, which purports to give an account of historical persons and events. Sometimes it relates the fortunes of empires; sometimes it degenerates into a mere genealogical tree. Every Javan "prince" has his "babad," in which the names of his ancestors and their deeds are recounted. Remembering the fertility of the Eastern imagination, and the despotic character of Eastern rulers, it is easy to understand that such babads were more often than not reduced in point of veracity to the standard of an average fairy tale. M. Brumund, whose remarks on this subject are embodied in Leemans' work on the Boro-Boedoer temple, deals very severely with the babads. He cannot away with them, and goes near to denying their claims for credence altogether. But surely a distinction should be made between the family babad, which is altered to suit the whims of a single prince, and those babads which relate events affecting the interests of several competing princes, or in which no single prince is especially interested. The Homeric poems, we are told, were kept reasonably free from interpolations by the jealousy of the various Hellenic communities. May not an influence of the same kind have operated in Java, and have preserved some of these chronicles from corruption?

That the babad is capable of being approached from two different points of view is apparent from the following extracts, in which I have compared M. Brumund's treatment of a babad of only fifty years ago with Mr. Nieman's account of an earlier babad in the possession of the Royal Asiatic Society.

M. Brumund says—

"Let us take, for example, Dhipa Negoro, the chief of the revolt in Java, which lasted until 1830; well, the babad represents him to us as enveloped in the clouds of the supernatural. There he is, surrounded by hundreds of enemies; he is about to be captured, but he calls to his aid the miraculous power which is at his disposal, and this power causes him to pass freely, safe and sound, through the threatening host, who suffer him to pass in their amazement, and who dare not even lift a finger against him. Another day he gives orders to have some cocoa-nut trees felled, and to have them covered with a white flag; he sets himself to pray, the flag is removed, and behold, the cocoa-nut trees are changed into pieces of artillery of the finest casting. He needs counsel; forthwith he is carried through the air to the southern shore and to the great spirit of the south, only to return forthwith after the conference. He wishes to pray at Mecca; scarcely has he formed the wish before his person is found upon the borders of the city, and, as a proof that he has really been there, he carries off a cake from the sacred city, all smoking hot."

Mangku Nagara, who is the subject of the babad discussed by Mr. Nieman, was a Javan prince who played a leading part, first in the Chinese war of 1745, and afterwards in the revolt of the Javan princes against the Dutch and the reigning susunan, known as "the Java war," which lasted from the close of the Chinese war to the year 1758. In the latter he fought for some time in alliance with Mangku Bumi, a younger brother of the susunan. After a time, however, this personage made terms with the Dutch on his own account, and Mangku Nagara, thus deserted, was compelled to submit to the susunan, and accept a modified territory for his administration. It was in this war that the Dutch obtained the deed of abdication mentioned in Chapter I. from the Susunan Pakubuona II., in the year 1849. The conduct of the war cost the company more than four million florins, but at its termination they had secured the virtual control of the island.

Mr. Nieman first gives some particulars about the manuscript.[28] It is entitled, he says, the "Babad Mangku Nagara." Its date is 1802; it is written in metre; its language is modern Javanese, but it contains some Kavi words, and one whole passage is written in the literary dialect. He then continues—

"Mangku Nagara is always depicted, not only as a brave and valiant, but also as a very religious man. His soldiers, and those of Mangku Bumi, who was at one time his ally, were steady adherents of the rites of Islam, so far as they were enabled to observe them, such as ablutions, prayer, the fast of Ramadan, and other practices of the Moslem. His confidence in the power of Allah, and his submission to his will when in distress, are praised, and his character is contrasted with that of the cruel Mangku Bumi, who put two of his wives to death for the most trifling offences, such as neglecting to offer him his coffee. Mangku Nagara, on the contrary, is described as greatly attached to his wives and children, carefully providing for their safety, and visiting them at their places of concealment, whenever he could snatch a temporary interval from his duties as a warrior. Attachment to his family, and attention to religious observances, seem to have been thought quite compatible with a strong attachment to the sex generally; we find him at the village of Zamenang, engaged for two months in copying the Koran and other religious works, and yet frequently amusing himself with the Bedaya, or dancing girls, from whom he was unable to separate himself in his retirement. Mangku Bumi had the impudence to deprive him of two of these women, whom he had previously presented to him as a mark of kindness; and, although he subsequently restored one of them to Mangku Nagara, the prince could not pardon the offence. The one that Mangku Bumi did not restore appears to have been especially a favourite of Mangku Nagara, whose grief and resentment were aggravated by some other offences; and the Dutch Governor of Samarang took advantage of this disposition to urge him to forsake the cause of Mangku Bumi. His efforts were at first successful, and Mangku Nagara made peace with the Dutch, and declared war against Mangku Bumi; but this state of things did not continue long. War soon recommenced between the Dutch and Mangku Nagara, from some cause which does not fully appear. It is believed that the latter was unable to prevent his adherents from quarrelling with and attacking the Dutch; but the fact is, the Mangku Bumi, finding himself unable to resist the united forces of Mangku Nagara and of the Dutch, found means to effect a reconciliation with the latter, and by their mediation received from the Susunan Zaku Buwana nearly a half of the Empire of Mataram, assumed the title of Sultan, and fixed his residence at Jotjokarta, the susunan residing at Solo, or Surakarta. This division of the empire took place in A.D. 1755. From this epoch the power of the unfortunate Mangku Nagara declined. Mangku Bumi made common cause with the Dutch and the susunan against him, and the desertion of several of his adherents, who now joined his relentless enemies, left him no rest. He was hunted from place to place like a wild beast, until he resolved, in his despair, to fall upon his numerous foes, in the persuasion that he should perish in the strife. Forty of his bravest friends joined in this resolution; their example encouraged the few troops who remained with him; they attacked their enemies with desperate courage, and unexpectedly gained a great victory. The Dutch were wholly defeated; nearly a hundred of them were left dead on the field of battle; and, better than all, his brave and indefatigable enemy, Van der Zoll, the Dutch commander, perished in the fight. Mangku Nagara's success, however, was not permanent; he was defeated in the next battle, and, although the war continued with varying success, sometimes to the advantage of one side, and sometimes of the other, his cause gradually declined. It was a guerilla war; Mangku Nagara was now flying to the mountains of Kerdenz, and now issuing forth to fall upon and harass his enemies; but upon the whole his losses were predominant, and the manuscript ends with an account of the peace he was compelled to submit to, and the conditions on which it was concluded. All this may be read in Raffles' "History."

The existence of such babads as this of Mangku Nagara would seem to point to the conclusion that a consecutive and reliable account of the Hindu period could be produced by careful sifting and comparison of the various babads dealing with this epoch. For this purpose they require to be examined by the methods of scientific history, and the results thus obtained must be checked by the faithful records of the antiquarian remains.

Among the prose works in modern Javanese, two, the "Niti Praja" and the "Surya Ngalam," are especially interesting as throwing light upon Javanese customs and thought. The former is one of a number of similar works, containing rules of conduct and instructions on points of Eastern etiquette especially intended for the information of the princes and nobility.

It is said to have been "compiled" by the Sultan Agung of Mataram. According to Vreede, the language of the "Niti Praja" is not Kavi, but it is written in the "stiff and artificial language common to the ethical treatises." The following passages are taken from translations which appear in Raffles' account of the work:—

"A good prince must protect his subjects against all unjust persecutions and oppressions, and should be the light of his subjects, even as the sun is the light of the world. His goodness must flow clear and full like the mountain stream, which, in its course towards the sea, enriches and fertilizes the land as it descends.

"When a prince gives audience to the public, his conduct must be dignified. He must sit upright, and not in a bending posture, and say little, neither looking on one side or the other, because, in this case, the people would not have a sight of him."

The following paragraph, which deals with the duty of a prime minister, is conceived in a spirit more suitable for the court of a constitutional monarch than for that of an Eastern potentate.

"It is a disgrace to a prime minister for any hostile attack to be made in the country entrusted to his charge without his knowledge, or that he should be careless or inattentive to the same, rather thinking how to obtain the favour of his prince than to secure the safety of the country."

An ambassador is directed to use all means within his power for obtaining information concerning the country to which he is sent. Then follow some directions which are specially characteristic of Eastern life.

"The letter must be carried on the shoulder, and in his gait and speech he must conduct himself with propriety. In delivering the letter he must present himself with dignity, approach first, and then retire from the person to whom the letter is directed, speak with him at a distance, and not too familiarly."

The "Surya Ngalam" is the most important of a group of legal treatises. Its author, or rather compiler, from whom it takes its title, was a Sultan of

Demak, the first of the Mohammedan states founded in Java. It is a compendium of Mohammedan law.

The modern version of the "Surya Ngalam" commences, "There was a certain raja of the West, named Sang Probu Suria Alem, who, being duly qualified, did, in the establishment of divine justice, frame a code of judicial regulations, consisting of one thousand five hundred and seven articles, which being afterwards digested and reduced to the number of one hundred and forty-four, were by him made known and explained to all the people of the countries under his authority, thereby diffusing knowledge and righteousness where ignorance and wickedness before prevailed."

I have already mentioned the jaksa,[29] as receiving information of offences, and sitting in the courts as assessor to the European judge-president. There are some very drastic punishments provided for this official in the section of the "Surya Ngalam" which treats of his duties.

"In the first place, he must possess a sufficient knowledge of the law, to know how to act in regard to cases which may come before him.... If the jaksa be found ignorant of these matters, he shall have his tongue cut out.... In the third place, any incorrect statement in writing shall be punished by the loss of both hands."

Among the modern Javanese works there appear a number of romances, of which the "Johar Manikam," which is taken from the Arabic, is an example. She was a sort of Javan Una, and the poem tells of her various deliverances from dangers, moral and physical. It commences with a sentence which is subtle enough for the nineteenth-century era. I quote this and the two following lines:—

"That is true love which makes the heart uneasy.
There was a woman who shone like a gem in the world, for she was distinguished by her conduct, and her name was Jowar Manikam.
Pure was her conduct like that of a saint, and she never forgot her devotions to the deity: all evil desires were strangers to her heart."

The dramatic works fall naturally into two divisions. The circle of poems, partly historical, which recount the adventures of Panji, the "knight" or national hero of Java, and which are called, after his name, "the Panjis;" and the wayang plays. The Panjis are important as alone supplying the Javan theatre with subjects for its representations. Among the titles of the various works included in the group are such as these: "The marriage of Panji and Angreni," "The History of the Lady Kurana, Princess of Bali," and "Panji and his Amours." There appears to be great uncertainty as to the origin and date of these poems. Vreede, after giving Raffles' account of the "Angrene"—the title under which the Panjis appear to have been then (1819) known—says that he has quoted the account of Raffles *verbatim* "because, notwithstanding the palpable inaccuracies of his conclusions, seeing our faulty information about the origin, the date, the authors, and the compilation of the Panji narratives, his indications may have, for all we know, great value."

As to the works directly due to the introduction of the Arabic language and literature simultaneously with the establishment of the Mohammedan power in the island, it is certainly remarkable, considering the completeness of the Mohammedan conquest and its long duration, that the Javanese language should show such few signs of Arabic influences as it does at the present time. The Koran was rendered into Javan verse a century and a half ago. Beside the various adaptations from the Arabic, there are a large number of Arabic treatises current in Java. Long ago Arabic schools were established in the island, and of these schools that in the district of Pranaraga at one time boasted of having as many as fifteen hundred scholars.

I shall conclude this account of the Javanese literature with a short description of the native theatre, and of the wayang.

As I have already mentioned, the subjects of the *topeng*, or Javan drama, are invariably taken from the group of Panji poems. The actors are dressed in the costumes of ancient times, and are gaudily decked with cheap jewellery, velvet, leather, and gold-embroidered cloths. A special characteristic of the native theatre is the fact that the actors wear masks and do not themselves speak, but the words of the play are recited by the dalang, or manager. The only occasion on which they depart from this practice is when the performance is given before one of the native princes, and in this case they also appear without their masks. In the performance of their somewhat limited functions they display considerable skill and histrionic capacity, but the piece resembles a ballet rather than a drama.[30] The recitations of the dalang are accompanied by the music of the gamelan, which, as in the case of the wayang, forms the orchestra. A topeng company numbers eleven persons—the dalang, six actors, and four gamelan musicians.

The subjects of the wayang plays are taken from the Kavi poems, from the Panjis, and especially from the chronicles. Some of these plays, or *lampahans*, are in metre, others are in prose. Both alike consist of summaries of the original poems on which they are based, and are intended for the use of the dalang. It is noticeable, however, that the wayang commands a far wider range of subjects than the theatre.

In the true wayang the figures themselves are not seen, but only their shadows. The dalang places a transparent curtain, stretched over a frame ten feet long by five high, between himself and the audience. He then fixes his figures in the bamboo bar immediately in front of him, and throws their shadows on to the curtain by placing a lamp behind them. At the same time he moves the arms with wires in order to produce the effect of action. The wayang dolls are singularly grotesque. There is an interesting tradition which ascribes this distortion to a deliberate purpose. According to this account, after the Mohammedan conquest and the subsequent conversion of the Javanese to Islamism, it became necessary to reconcile the continued enjoyment of the national pastime with the precept of the new religion which forbade the dramatic representation of the human form. A means of escaping from the dilemma was discovered by the susunan of that day, who ordered the wayang figures to be distorted to their present grotesque shapes. His line of argument was ingenious. The world, he said, would now no longer recognize the figures of the wayang as representations of humanity. The Javanese, however, would recognize the persons whom the figures were intended to reproduce from their knowledge of the national traditions. Even if *they* should eventually come to forget the nature of the originals good would arise, for they would then believe that it was only since their conversion to the faith of the prophet that their ancestors had assumed a human shape.

There are two forms of the shadow wayang, the *purva* and the *gedog*. The subjects of the first are taken from the various mythological works of the Hindu period, and from the Bharata Yuddha. In presenting this wayang, the dalang first recites a few verses in Kavi, and then continues the narrative in a modern Javanese version. This wayang is especially useful as serving to keep alive some knowledge of the literary dialect among the common people. The wayang gedog differs from the former in so far as its subjects belong to a later period, and no Kavi verses are recited. The gamelan also which accompanies the dalang is somewhat different. Pangi is the favourite hero of the wayang gedog, though he is not represented so exclusively as in the theatre. In both of these wayangs the dalang often improvises the dialogue with which the narrative is interspersed.

I have described the wayang klitik in my account of my visit to Tji Wangi. The performance is given without the intervention of a curtain, and the figures in the wayang are slightly smaller and not nearly so skilfully constructed as in the two former. The wayang klitik takes its subjects from the period of the Mohammedan invasion.

The dalangs are held in great respect by the common people, and many of them possess their own sets of wayang puppets. It is customary for the native princes to keep a dalang at their palaces; in this case, of course, the figures and gamelan do not belong to the dalang, but to the prince.

A WAYANG FIGURE.

Footnotes:

[28] *Journal of the R. A. S.* xx. 1863.

[29] In Chapter III.

[30] See p. 56.

CHAPTER XV.
SINGAPORE.

Batavia and Singapore—Raffles' arrival in the East— Determines to oppose the Dutch supremacy in the Archipelago—Occupation of Java—Is knighted—Returns from England—Foundation of Singapore—Uncertainty whether the settlement would be maintained—His death—Description of Singapore—Epilogue.

A fortnight after my visit to Tji Wangi I left Java. As the train took us from Batavia to the port, I caught a glimpse of the sea over the palm-trees, and I felt something of the exultation which prompted the remnant of the ten thousand Greeks to exclaim, "The sea! the sea!" I had tired of the steamy atmosphere of Batavia, and that line of blue seemed full of revivifying power. Three days later we reached Singapore. Here everything was bright and new and English—miles of wharfs crowded with shipping, broad streets, the cathedral spire *en evidence*, tall warehouses, and handsome Government buildings. Watering-carts replaced the bamboo buckets in the streets, and English iron and stone work the quaint lamps and antiquated masonry. There the Dutch lived by themselves; the wide streets, education, Christianity, were for them exclusively. Here it was otherwise. Even the native streets were well drained and lighted; for the Englishman shares his civilization with the native races. The glory of the place is its splendidly turfed and tree-clad esplanade; and in the centre of the broad carriage-road there stands the statue of Sir Stamford Raffles, for five years Lieutenant-Governor of Java and the founder of Singapore.

The British occupation of Singapore arose so directly out of the cession of Java, that a description of the circumstances which led to this event will suitably complete my account of that country.

THE ESPLANADE, SINGAPORE.

After some years' service as a clerk in the East India house in London, Raffles was despatched in 1805, when only twenty-three years of age, to the East, as assistant-secretary to the Government of Penang, where a settlement was then being formed by the company. In this capacity he so distinguished himself as to attract the notice of Lord Minto, then Governor-General of India. In particular Raffles made himself acquainted, as no other European had done before, with the circumstances and character of the Malay races. Subsequently, in view of the annexation of Holland by Napoleon, it became desirable for the Indian Government to take some measures to prevent the establishment of the French in the Dutch possessions in the East. When, as a means to this end, it was determined to occupy Java, it was to Raffles that Lord Minto applied for the necessary information upon which the operations of the expedition could be based. The capture of Java was considered of such importance that the Governor-General himself accompanied the expedition. Raffles' information was found to be so accurate, and his suggestions so valuable, that after the capitulation of General Jansens on September 18, 1811, Lord Minto entrusted the island to his charge. Up to the present, Raffles had been acting first as agent and afterwards as chief secretary to the Governor-General; he was now appointed Lieutenant-Governor of Java and its dependencies.

I have already written of the principles upon which Raffles based his measures during the five years of his administration, and of the criticism which was directed against them. The whole of Raffles' public acts as a servant of the company were reviewed by the Court of Directors in 1826. The verdict of this very competent authority, with reference to the financial expedients and the general reforms which he adopted in his administration of the island, was entirely favourable, if we except what refers to the sale of lands, which it characterized as a "questionable proceeding." It is worthy of note, however, that this "questionable proceeding" had been pronounced by the Governor-General to be "an able expedient in a moment of great emergency." Raffles was bitterly disappointed when the news reached him that, under the settlement effected by the Treaty of London, the British Government had consented to restore Java to the Dutch. For a moment the announcement of Napoleon's escape from Elba seemed to bring a chance of a reprieve. But this transient gleam of hope was soon dispelled, and in March, 1816, Raffles relinquished the government to the imperial officer appointed to carry out the transference of the island. Lord Minto had secured for him the residency of Bencoolen, a settlement on the western coast of Sumatra; but his state of health was so unsatisfactory that it became necessary for him to proceed to England without delay.

After a stay of only fifteen months' duration, during which he received the honour of knighthood from the king, Raffles again set sail for India in

October, 1817. He was appointed to the government of Bencoolen, with the title of Lieutenant-Governor of Fort Marlborough, and it is in this capacity that he signed his Singapore proclamations. It appears, however, that he was in some way commissioned by the Home Government to exercise a general supervision over British interests in the further East. In a letter written in 1820 he says that he "had separate instructions from the Court to watch the motions of foreign nations, and particularly the Dutch, in the Archipelago generally, and to write to the Court and the Secret Committee."[31] On his arrival at Bencoolen in March, 1819, he set himself once more to achieve that object for which he had incessantly worked ever since his first appearance in the East—the establishment of British influence in Malaya and the Eastern Archipelago. With this object in view Raffles resolved to proceed to Calcutta, in order that he might personally confer with Lord Hastings, who had succeeded Lord Minto as Governor-General, and secure the co-operation of the Bengal Government in his plans. He arrived at Calcutta early in July of the same year. Lord Hastings expressed a high appreciation of the value of Raffles' services in Java, and gave him general assurances of his further support. Although the Bengal Government were not prepared to endorse the extension of the British authority in Sumatra, they and the British merchants at Calcutta were at least rendered sensible by Raffles' arguments of the importance of endeavouring to check the progress of the Dutch in the Malay Peninsula. Of the two channels which alone gave access to the Archipelago, one was already in the hands of the Dutch, and the other soon would be. In short, unless some immediate and energetic measures were taken, the trade of the whole Eastern Archipelago would be closed against the English merchants. In his own words, Raffles asked for neither territory nor people; all he wanted was "permission to anchor a line-of-battle ship and hoist the English flag."

In short, the result of Raffles' visit to Calcutta was that the Bengal Government resolved, if possible, to keep the command of the Straits of Malacca, and he was despatched as their agent to effect this purpose.

It appears that the Bengal Government hoped to sufficiently command the straits by an establishment at Achin, in the extreme north of Sumatra, and by taking possession of Rhio, a small island south of Singapore. Raffles, however, foresaw—what indeed happened—that the Dutch would anticipate him in the occupation of Rhio, while Achin seemed scarcely suitable for the purpose. When he left Calcutta he had another plan in view. On December 12, 1818, he writes from on board the *Nearchus*, at the mouth of the Ganges, to his frequent correspondent Marsden, the Sumatran traveller—

"We are now on our way to the eastward, in the hope of doing something, but I much fear the Dutch have hardly left us an inch of ground to stand upon. My attention is principally turned to Johore, and you must not be surprised if my next letter to you is dated from the site of the ancient city of Singapura."

In carrying out the difficult task which had been entrusted to him, Raffles encountered not only the opposition of the Dutch, which he naturally expected, but that of the Government of Penang. The authorities at Penang had a double reason for their opposition. In the first place, they regarded the establishment of a station further east as detrimental to the interests of their own settlement; and, in the next, they had themselves unsuccessfully endeavoured to acquire a similar position, and now maintained that the time had gone by for such measures. Fortunately, however, Raffles had already secured the services of Colonel Farquhar and a military force. This officer was in command of the troops at Bencoolen, which, at the time Raffles left Calcutta, were on the point of being relieved. Raffles had written from Calcutta, instructing him to proceed to Europe by the Straits of Sunda, where he would receive further instructions.

Singapore, the spot which Raffles' knowledge of the Malay states enabled him to secure for his settlement, is a small island, twenty-seven miles long by fourteen broad, immediately south of the Malay Peninsula, from which it is separated by a channel of less than a mile in width. No situation could be imagined better calculated to secure the objects which the new settlement was intended to effect. Not only does the island completely command the Straits of Malacca, the gate of the ocean highway to China and the Eastern Archipelago, but, lying at a convenient distance from the Chinese, the Indian, and the Javanese ports, it was admirably adapted to serve as an *entrepôt* and centre of English trade.

The island at this time formed part of the territory of the Sultan of Johore, and it contained the remains of the original maritime capital of the Malays. It was within the circuit of these Malay fortifications, raised more than six centuries ago, that, on the 29th of February, 1819, Raffles planted the British flag at Singapore.

From the very first Raffles fully realized the value of the acquisition. On the 19th of February, 1819, he writes that he has found "at Singapore advantages far superior to what Rhio afforded." And in the same letter he says, "In short, Singapore is everything we could desire, and I may consider myself most fortunate in the selection; it will soon rise into importance, and with this single station alone, I would undertake to counteract all the plans of Mynheer."

Raffles was not able to remain for more than a few days at Singapore. He hurried on to Achin, and, after completing the object of his mission there, returned to his residency at Bencoolen. But the new settlement rapidly progressed under Colonel Farquhar's able administration. A year afterwards, this officer writes to Raffles that "nothing can possibly exceed the rising trade and general prosperity of this infant colony." He adds, "Merchants of all descriptions are collecting here so fast that nothing is heard in the shape of complaint but the want of more ground to build on."

In spite of this immediate assurance of prosperity, it remained for a long time uncertain whether the British Government would maintain the settlement.

The right of possession was from the first disputed by the Dutch. Raffles himself succinctly states in a letter to Marsden the basis upon which this rested. It appears, from his letter, that the Dutch had secured the cession of Rhio from the Sultan of Lingen, whom they recognized as the Sultan of Johore. On his arrival at Singapore, Raffles was visited by one of the two chief hereditary officials of Johore, who represented to him that an elder brother of the Sultan of Lingen was the legal successor to that throne, adding, that as the Dutch had negotiated with an incompetent authority, it was still open to the English to effect a settlement on the territory of Johore. This elder brother was subsequently recognized by the nobles at the court of Johore, and it was with this personage, in his capacity of Sultan of Johore, that Raffles concluded his treaty, and obtained permission to establish his settlement. The Dutch, on the other hand, maintained that the Sultan of Lingen had been legally invested with the sovereignty of Johore at the time of the occupation; and, therefore, that the permission accorded to Raffles was worthless. In a letter bearing date July 19, 1820, a correspondent writes to him from London—

"You are probably aware of the obstacles which have been opposed to the adoption of your measures, and even threatened your position in the service. Your zeal considerably out-stepped your prudence, and the first operations of it became known at an unfavourable juncture. It was thought that the state of affairs in Europe required that they should be discountenanced.

"The acquisition of Singapore has grown in importance. The stir made here lately for the further enlargement of the Eastern trade fortified that impression. It is now accredited in the India House."[32]

Undoubtedly the Dutch were making strong endeavours at this time to procure the removal from the East of a man who had shown himself so resolute and capable an opponent of their commercial system. Raffles himself writes from Bencoolen in July, 1820, "After all, it is not impossible the ministry may be weak enough to abandon Singapore, and to sacrifice me, honour, and the Eastern Archipelago to the outrageous pretensions of the Dutch." Fortunately he had powerful friends, and he was not immediately recalled. Meanwhile he continued to hold the settlement on his personal responsibility against the efforts of both the British and Dutch East India Governments. In eighteen months it had grown from an insignificant fishing village to a port with a population of 10,000 inhabitants. During the first two and a half years of its existence Singapore was visited by as many as 2889 vessels, with an aggregate burden of 161,515 tons. The total value of its exports and imports for the year 1822 amounted to no less than 8,568,172 dollars.[33]

Raffles returned to Singapore on the 10th of October, 1822, on his way to England. He remained in the settlement for nine months, and during this time employed himself in laying-out the city, and in drawing up rules and regulations for the government of its people. In one of his letters he expresses a hope "that, though Singapore may be the first capital established in the nineteenth century, it will not disgrace the brightest period of it."

The position of Raffles in respect to Singapore was indeed remarkable. Though a servant of the company for five years, he was personally responsible for the administration of the settlement, and neither the Bengal Government nor the Court of Directors in London would relieve him. In the report which he sent to the Bengal Government before returning to England, he states the main principles upon which he has based the regulations which he framed. At the head of them stands a declaration of the principle of free trade.

"First I have declared that the port of Singapore is a free port, and the trade thereof open to ships and vessels of every nation, free of duty, equally and alike to all." It was a hatred of their monopolist policy which had especially inspired Raffles in his opposition to the Dutch. In respect of the question of the authority of his legislation, he writes that he considered himself justified in thus provisionally legislating for the settlement by reason of the existence of "an actual and urgent necessity for some immediate and provisional arrangements." He further states that in framing these regulations he has, while giving due weight to local considerations, "adhered as closely as possible to those principles which from immemorial usage have ever been considered the most essential and sacred parts of the British constitution."

Before he left Singapore, Raffles selected twelve merchants and appointed them to act as magistrates for a year. He also provided for a succession of such magistrates, who were to be chosen from a list kept by the Resident.

Raffles' career was cut short by his sudden and premature death, which took place on the 5th of July, 1826. He had lived, however, long enough to see the merit of his public conduct established by the judgment of the Court of Directors, which I have already mentioned, and which was pronounced in the preceding April. The fortunes of Singapore were secured two years previously to this event, when the island was formally ceded to the British Government by the Sultan of Johore, in pursuance of the terms of an arrangement then concluded between the Dutch and English Governments. Subsequently it formed part of the consolidated Government of Penang, Singapore, and Malacca. In 1867 these settlements were converted into a Crown colony under the name of the Straits Settlements. At the present time the colony so constituted is administered by a Governor, and an Executive Council of eight members, assisted by a Legislative Council consisting of these eight official, and seven other unofficial, members.

The town of Singapore has fully realized the expectations of its founder. Its rapid and continuous growth is sufficiently indicated by the fact that at the present time it possesses a population of 182,650 inhabitants; while the importance of its trade is demonstrated by the fact that more than three million tons of shipping entered the port in the year 1889. In connection with the growing recognition of the necessity for an organized system of naval defence for the empire, the strategical value of Singapore has of late years been greatly emphasized, and the defences of the port have been strengthened and improved. Batteries have been constructed by the colony at a cost of £100,000, which have been furnished with guns at the expense of the Imperial Government. At the same time a new harbour, including the Tanjong Pagar wharf and docks, has been added three miles to the westward, where the largest ocean-going steamships can find ample space.

The original "fort" is still conspicuous in the centre of the town, and behind it are the gently rising hills on which the bungalows of the English residents are for the most part built. At evening the blinds are drawn up to welcome the reviving breath of the sea, and from the open windows of these bungalows appears a panoramic scene of singular extent and beauty, and one which forms a fitting background to the Eastern viands and Chinese servants which give a Singapore dinner-party a character of its own.

THE CAVANAGH BRIDGE, SINGAPORE.

The ricsha furnishes the streets with an additional element of picturesqueness. These charming vehicles are not used, however, by Europeans during the day. Then the Anglo-Saxon instinct for respectability (or some more subtle reason) prescribes the use of the ghari, which is practically a four-wheeled cab with Venetian blinds substituted for windows. The ricsha is especially used by the Chinese, who, as in Java, have contrived to get most of the retail trade into their hands, and many of whom are extremely wealthy and greatly attached to the British connection. In addition to the public offices, the most noticeable buildings are the Government House, which stands on a slight elevation and is surrounded by a park, the cathedral, and the Raffles Museum. Near the Cavanagh Bridge—a handsome iron suspension bridge which spans the river—is the hospitable and commodious Singapore club; and just outside the town there is a fine race-course. The esplanade together with this latter provide the English residents with the means of outdoor recreation which are so essential in the tropics. I have already spoken of the great advantage which Singapore possesses over Batavia in the singular healthiness of its climate. Almost the first sight which I saw on my arrival was that of an English crowd surrounding the tennis courts on the esplanade, where a very considerable tournament was proceeding. It is by such pursuits as these, polo, golf, cricket, and tennis, that the insidious languor of the East can alone be resisted.

There are times when, among the prosaic surroundings of this work-a-day world, our senses are unexpectedly stirred by some undetected stimulus which sets in motion a train of memories. Such memories penetrate even the gloomy recesses of Temple chambers. Sometimes they bring with them a waft of perfume from the warm pine woods that clothe the slopes of Table Mountain; sometimes a vision of glassy waters walled by the sheer mountain heights of New Zealand Sounds; or it may be a sense of calm swan-like motion over the sunlit reaches of the Hawkesbury. Not least interesting among such memories I count the recollection of a time when life was lived on a verandah, in the twilight of palm leaves, and its needs were served by dusky ministers whose footfall brought no disturbing sound.

It is not so very long ago since Mr. Lucy wrote that a man in search of "pastures new" might do worse than try Japan. I would add that, having tried Japan (and who has not?), he might do worse than take to Java. Here, in an island where the business of the great world is heard only as the murmur of a neighbouring stream, he will find an ancient and interesting civilization still existing, some vast Hindu ruins, and the gardens of Buitenzorg.

Footnotes:

[31] "Memoir of Sir Stamford Raffles, by his widow." 1830.

[32] "Memoir of Sir Stamford Raffles."

[33] The Mexican dollar, which varies in value, but is worth about four shillings.

www.ingramcontent.com/pod-product-compliance
Ingram Content Group UK Ltd.
Pitfield, Milton Keynes, MK11 3LW, UK
UKHW030057050125
3900UKWH00005B/864